W9-BKW-891

Southerners

INSTITUTE FOR RESEARCH IN SOCIAL SCIENCE
MONOGRAPH SERIES

Published by The University of North Carolina Press
in association with the Institute for Research in Social Science
at The University of North Carolina at Chapel Hill

Southerners

The Social Psychology of

Sectionalism

John Shelton Reed

The University of North Carolina Press

Chapel Hill

© 1983 The University of North Carolina Press

All rights reserved

Manufactured in the United States of America

Library of Congress Cataloging in Publication Data

Reed, John Shelton.
Southerners: The Social Psychology of Sectionalism

(Institute for Research in Social Science monograph
series)
Bibliography: p.
Includes index.
1. Southern States—Civilization—Public opinion.
2. Sectionalism (United States)—Public opinion.
3. Public opinion—Southern States. I. Title.
II. Series.
F216.2.R44 1983   306'.0975   82-13631
ISBN 0-8078-1542-X
ISBN 0-8078-4098-X pbk.

To Herbert Hyman,
for lessons in survey research,
and in Northern hospitality

CONTENTS

FIGURES AND TABLES

PREFACE

When the opportunity arose in 1971 to include a number of questions about the South and Southerners in a statewide survey that was being conducted by the Institute for Research in Social Science at the University of North Carolina, Glen Elder and I saw it as a chance to check out some ideas we had been discussing about the similarity of white Southerners to American immigrant and racial groups. We thought it would be a good opportunity to develop measures that we could use in some later Southwide or even nationwide survey. Consequently, in the short time we had available, we collected an odd lot of questionnaire items that had been used in the study of various ethnic groups, changed the referent from whatever it had been to "Southerners," and threw them into the survey. The result, I am afraid, was a somewhat haphazard assortment of items and some poorly measured concepts.

Still, the survey broke new ground. Survey researchers had not asked Southerners this sort of question before. As the results came in, we read them with fascination, and our preliminary analyses of the data suggested that we were onto something very interesting. But, for a variety of complicated and uninteresting reasons, we never got around to doing the anticipated full-dress inquiry. Data from the 1971 survey found their way into a number of seminar papers and dissertations (most of them cited here), and I have often cited or referred to unpublished findings from the survey myself, but most of the data and analysis reported here have not previously been published.[1]

As time passed, both Glen Elder and I moved on to other projects (and Glen to other parts of the country), and it became clear that we would not—at least, not soon—do it *right*, so I began to

1. See Reed, *One South*.

work, off and on, on this report. Returning to the analysis of this survey after such an interval and with a different purpose in mind from the basically experimental aims that we started with, I have found myself, again and again, wondering why "they" measured something as they did or why "they" failed to measure something of obvious importance—only to be brought up short by the recollection that I was one of "them." I beg methodologically inclined readers, in their charity, to think of this as something of an exercise in secondary analysis (or at least what Herbert Hyman has called "semi-secondary" analysis), with all of the problems that attend that approach.[2] To avoid tedium, I have probably not hedged and qualified as much as I should, but I hope that this disclaimer will warn readers of the data's limitations and indicate that I am aware of them.

For all that, when I began to work on these materials for publication, it seemed to me (and it still does) that, even though the measurement is not ideal, the sample a constricted one, and the survey now approaching adolescence, a better survey conducted today would not materially alter the conclusions I have reached about the ways in which these social-psychological variables are related to one another, although it would let us explore them in more detail and with greater precision. I hope these data will demonstrate both that this is a useful approach to the study of the South and that the study of American regional groups can illuminate more general issues in the study of intergroup relations. Finally, I hope very much that I have managed to recapture some of the excitement we felt as we began to listen to what these North Carolinians had to say about the South and their relationship with it.

John Shelton Reed
Bellagio, Italy
August 1981

2. Hyman, *Secondary Analysis of Sample Surveys*.

ACKNOWLEDGMENTS

An absurdly large number of people contributed to the writing and publication of this short book, and I am grateful to them all. My colleague and friend, Glen Elder, now of Cornell University, was a more than equal partner in the formulation of the original survey questions and in our preliminary data analysis, and I would have insisted that he be the senior author of anything the two of us wrote together. As things worked out, we did not write anything jointly, and I have taken these data in new and perhaps strange directions, so Glen may not care to share responsibility for my conclusions. But he cannot escape credit for this inquiry's beginnings, and the conclusions would have been impossible without his contribution. I appreciate his patronage of one who was the most junior of junior faculty, a patronage so gracious that I never thought of it that way at the time.

I wish also to thank the National Science Foundation, whose grant (GU-2059) supported the "Survey of North Carolina" (and me, for part of a summer), and the staff at the Institute for Research in Social Science who conducted the survey and allowed us to "piggyback" our questions about the South onto it. Angell Beza, director of the survey, was unfailingly helpful and cooperative, and Appendix A is his doing. The institute's field staff did a superb job, scrupulously recording responses to our many open-ended questions, judging how "Southern" respondents' accents were, and providing much valuable information in the form of notes at the end of the interview schedule. The technical staff of the institute, particularly the staff of its data library, did their usual fine job of providing whatever help was asked for and some we did not know enough to ask for.

Obviously, survey researchers are indebted to their respondents, and in this case perhaps the debt is even greater than usual. I would like to thank the thousand or so respondents who each gave over an hour and a half (and in most cases, as the responses indicate, a good deal of thought) to our questions. That many of them even thanked our interviewers and said they had enjoyed the interview is Southern hospitality indeed.

Three research assistants deserve special thanks as well. Cynthia Kenyon (now Chirot) earned my great respect and gratitude by working as a coder on some of the verbatim material we had gathered. An undergraduate then, she volunteered to do it without pay, "for the experience," and she has since gone on (as I knew she would) to greater things. Pamela Oliver was an able and conscientious research assistant, patiently shepherding our data through the preliminary computer runs, but her major contribution was in helping us to think about what the computer was producing. She may not remember those conversations, but I do. When, in 1981, I came back to these data after some years, Steve Lerner did a heroic job of tracking down fugitive documentation and rerunning all of the tables to verify that I had found what I thought I had found.

Several students, of whom Pam was one, have used the data from the "Survey of North Carolina" in papers and dissertations. I have profited from these, as well as from the work of some of our other students, as my bibliography attests. I want to thank them here, especially Harold Grasmick, whose measure of the "traditional value orientation" I have simply pirated for use in chapter 3. Thanks also to the students from my undergraduate research methods course who helped me to carry out the survey of Carolina undergraduates reported in chapter 6.

In preparing the manuscript, I had the invaluable assistance of Bonnie Samuelson and Ellen McLamb, who typed it, and of Sarah Sherer, who patiently initiated me into the mysteries of the ABDick Magna SL.

Alvin Bertrand, Ernest Campbell, and Miles Simpson read the first draft of my manuscript. The final version was better for their suggestions and would have been better still had I taken more of them. Mary Ellen Marsden, at the Institute for Research in Social

Science, and Iris Hill, at the University of North Carolina Press, both took personal interest in the project and provided encouragement at least as important as their editorial counsel.

For permission to reprint the figures on pages 46 and 98, I am grateful to *Social Forces*, whose former editor, Everett Wilson, has always been a percipient and constructive critic, as well as a friend. Everett serves as a "reader over my shoulder"—sometimes literally, but often, as in this book, figuratively: his real or imagined comments keep me from succumbing altogether to my native Southern tendency to particularism.

Finally, I thank the Rockefeller Foundation for the opportunity to write this monograph in the salubrious setting of the Villa Serbelloni on Lake Como; the villa's staff for being so attentive to my needs and whims that I could find no excuse for *not* writing; my parents and parents-in-law for keeping their grandchildren; Elisabeth and Sarah, for being themselves; and Dale, as always.

Southerners

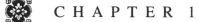

CHAPTER 1

Introduction

It has been a long time since Jonathan Daniels wrote that, "For good or for ill, being a Southerner is like being a Jew. And, indeed, more needs to be written about the similarity of the minds and the emotions of the Jew, the Irishman, the Southerner, and, perhaps, the Pole, as a basis for the better understanding of each of them and of them all."[1] But sometime in the late 1960s, in the context of the "ethnic revival" of those years, several social scientists independently began to look into the analogy that Daniels had suggested.[2] A variety of evidence had accumulated to indicate that, although the culture of the South was indeed changing, it was by no means disappearing as a distinctive variation on the basic American theme.[3] The concurrent rediscovery of the vitality of American immigrant cultures suggested, if not an explanation, at least a context for explanation—a more general category of unexpected phenomena into which the Southern case might be fitted.

This was, in some ways, a new departure for social scientists interested in the South. Looking not so much at *the South* as at *Southerners*, and treating them as one of the many "primordial" groups that make up the pluralistic society of the United States, these scholars were obliged to take seriously the ordinary concerns of ethnic group research—questions of identity, stereo-

1. Quoted in Tindall, *The Ethnic Southerners*, p. 11.
2. See especially Killian, *White Southerners*; Reed, "Southerners" and *The Enduring South*; and Greeley, *Ethnicity in the United States*.
3. See below, pp. 108–10.

typing, prejudice, social distance, and the like—and to see how well the analogy fit. These topics had been not only ignored but purposely avoided by earlier generations of social science "regionalists," on the grounds that to study them would be divisive.[4] (Historians and literary scholars had not ignored them, to be sure, but most of their work was in a different idiom and required some translation to make its relevance apparent to social scientists.)

These inquiries generally supported the basic assumption that it was indeed worthwhile to apply the conceptual and methodological apparatus of ethnic group research to the study of Southerners. Although some of the differences between Southerners and groups more commonly thought of as "ethnic" are obvious (and others, less obvious, need to be emphasized), there are enough similarities to suggest that searching for others might be a productive line of work. This monograph is an essay in that direction.

The Data and Their Limitations

Most of the data here come from the responses of white North Carolinians to a number of questions that Glen Elder and I included in the 1971 general population survey of North Carolina described in Appendix A. Many of the questions were adapted from items used in the study of other ethnic groups; a few were written especially for this inquiry. As recently as that, we (like most other Americans, I believe) construed "Southerners" to mean *white* Southerners, and it struck us as possibly puzzling or offensive to ask black respondents some of our key questions. Looking at the responses to those questions we did ask blacks, which are presented in Appendix B, I now believe that our decision was a mistake. I have tried to make what amends I can in that appendix. Robert Sherer has analyzed some of those responses elsewhere, and the title of his paper, "I'm from Dixie, Too," tells the story.[5]

4. See Reed, *One South*, chap. 2, "Whatever Became of Regional Sociology?"
5. The relatively small number of black respondents (slightly over 200) pre-

Since our purpose was not precise statistical description (which would give us, at best, a quantitative portrait of attitudes and beliefs in one Southern state in 1971) but rather to look into the fundamental nature and underlying dimensions of regional identity, we included a great many open-ended questions, asking respondents to answer in their own words and often to tell us why they had answered as they did. Our interviewers attempted to record these responses verbatim.

It is obvious from the material we got that some respondents had given the subject a lot of thought and were just waiting to share their conclusions with somebody. Others had not thought about it much, but responded enthusiastically to the invitation to do so, and gave us some valuable material. A few, inevitably, found the enterprise mystifying from beginning to end. That was all right with us: in fact, we used this variation in what we came to call "regional consciousness" as one of our key variables. In any case, there was no indication in the responses or in our "debriefing" of the interviewers that anyone found our part of the interview *boring*.

Obviously, we would have preferred a Southwide sample to one composed entirely of North Carolinians, and a nationwide sample to a Southwide one. We would like to have been able to look at migrants from the South, who are, our data suggest, a particularly interesting group. Moreover, it appears that the attitudes of *non-Southerners* have a great deal to do with what Southerners believe about themselves: we can look at what Southerners think non-Southerners think about Southerners (if you follow that), but without a sample of non-Southerners we cannot examine their attitudes directly.

---

cluded detailed attention to variation within the black population, in any case, and there is also some evidence that black attitudes toward the South were changing rapidly at the time of the survey. At just about that time, net migration for blacks reversed its historic pattern (for the first time, more native-born blacks entered the South than left it), and this behavior was accompanied by a reassessment of "Southerners": by 1976 black Southerners felt as "warm" toward them as did white Southerners, that is to say, very warm indeed. See Merle Black and John Shelton Reed, "Blacks and Southerners," in Reed, *One South*, chap. 8.

Still, if the study must be restricted to a single state, there is a great deal to be said for the state of North Carolina. If not a typical Southern state (which one is?), it at least includes nearly all of the important types of Southern communities. There are mountain counties with Unionist and Republican histories and negligible black populations; cotton-growing, "Deep South" counties in the east, with black majorities; rural, tobacco-growing counties, industrial and commercial towns and cities, and white-collar suburbs in the piedmont. There are communities with econ-omies based on tourism, counties supported by military bases, and towns where universities and research institutions are the ma-jor employers. Some counties have been losing population for decades; others have undergone rapid urbanization, attracting mi-grants from all over the Southeast and from outside the region altogether. In short, most economically and demographically sig-nificant variation within the South as a whole can be found within the state (the exceptions, of course, being those interesting but troublesome communities on the fringe of the region—the South-west, south Florida, and northern Virginia). Although I would hesitate to generalize from our sample statistics to the regional ones, because the sample is certainly not representative of the entire South, it is less important for our present purposes that the sample be representative than that it be inclusive—and it proba-bly is that.

The sample is "unrepresentative" in another way as well: it was drawn in 1971 and a great deal has happened since then. In partic-ular, we have evidence to show that (as one could have predicted, and some did, in 1971) white Southern attitudes have continued to change in those areas connected with what we shall call the "tra-ditional value orientation." Support for segregation has continued to erode, anti-Semitism and anti-Catholicism have continued to decline, sex-role attitudes have been slowly changing, and no doubt other related changes have escaped the attention of poll-sters, or anyway *my* attention. There are, as well, the impondera-ble effects of the election of a Southern president, amid all the signs of an era of good feeling that encompassed not only the

Carter family and staff but also Sam Ervin and Burt Reynolds.[6] To be sure, the man was not reelected, and we have some evidence that his election did not fundamentally affect Northern attitudes toward Southerners, but whether it affected Southerners' views of themselves—in particular, their sense of being excluded and condescended to—is a question we simply cannot address with these data.[7]

I suspect, however, that although the *levels* of some of the variables we examine have changed, their *relationships* have not. It may be, that is, that fewer Southerners now feel that "Northerners have more power in Washington than is fair," but it seems likely that believing that is still related to regional identification. In any case, I have not made a great deal in the text of the absolute levels of our variables: they are affected not only by *when* they were asked but by *where* (the sample is only of North Carolinians) and *how* (question-wording effects are often quite large). Patterns of relationships among variables should be much less sensitive to these essentially uninteresting sources of variation.

Theoretical Underpinnings

The theoretical orientation that guided the development of the questions we asked and that underlies my organization and presentation of these results is that of field theory, as formulated by the social psychologist Kurt Lewin.[8] Those who are familiar with Lewin's work will, I hope, recognize the use I have made of it here. I have tried to be unobtrusive about it: I am not "testing"

6. On "Southern-fried chic," see Tindall, "The Sunbelt Snow Job," and Vanover, "The Useful South."

7. Pierce, "Jimmy Carter and the New South."

8. See his *Field Theory in Social Science*. Most of these questions could also be framed in terms of "attribution theory" and its concern with "lay epistemology"—how human beings as "naïve scientists" attempt to deal with the world of experience. For examples of this approach, see Harvey, Ickes, and Kidd, *New Directions in Attribution Research*.

field theory, merely using it as a sort of scaffolding to construct this inquiry, and scaffolding is not ordinarily left in place when the job is finished. In this introduction, however, it may be appropriate to sketch some of the features of field theory (omitting Lewin's efforts to mathematize it) and to indicate its relation to the outline of this work, for anyone who happens to be interested.

Lewin's concern, and mine, is with the individual's "life space" (his cognitive field or psychological environment), that is, with his environment *as he sees it* and with the properties and relations of entities within it. Obviously, people's representations of their environment reflect, in most cases, the realities of their physical and social surroundings; but those representations will also be shaped by what and how individuals have been taught to perceive, their characteristic ways of seeing and organizing what they see, and their needs, moods, goals, ideals, and so forth. In consequence, someone's cognitive representation of objects in the "real world" (including social "objects" like regional groups) may be more or less detailed, more or less subject to modification by experience, more or less accurate.

I have tried here to investigate the place and role of the concept "Southerners" in the life spaces of the North Carolinians we interviewed. We need to ask a number of questions. In the first place, does the group *exist* for a given respondent; does it occupy a space in his cognitive field? If so, what does it "look" like? Are its boundaries well-defined, or does it shade off gradually into non-Southerners? Are its boundaries permeable in either direction? How different is it, and in what ways, from its surroundings? Is it differentiated internally and, if so, how? Is it a conventional representation, that is, does it look like other people's? Is it what is often called a "stereotype" (a term usually reserved for exaggeratedly different, insufficiently discriminating, widely shared, and derogatory representations)? What sorts of factors (for a sociologist, what sorts of experiences and background factors) affect the answers to these questions?

We can be certain that the answers to these questions will be affected by and will affect whether someone sees the group as one that *includes him*. If the word "Southerner" means anything to an individual, what determines whether he thinks of himself as one? When people see a group as excluding them, is this because they see themselves as lacking some necessary qualification for membership? If so, what do they regard as necessary? Is it the case that some who might regard themselves as eligible choose not to belong, perhaps because they dislike the group? Or is membership not seen as a matter of choice?

We can think of the forces that attract someone to a group or repel him from it (dislike is one of the latter). Lewin wrote of "valences," vectors representing the sum of these forces, and we can also think of the valence of cognitive regions *outside* the group. If the group's boundaries are seen as permeable (that is, if the group can be entered and left), one will ordinarily "move" until these forces are in equilibrium. One will, in other words, love it or (psychologically) leave it. These valences are usually based on beliefs—on *cognition* (for example, of one's similarity to members of the group or of one's dependence on them). But they are by nature *affective*, partaking of evaluation, admiration, "good feeling."

The usefulness of thinking in these terms can be illustrated, it seems to me, by considering what it means to say that people *identify* with a group. In these terms, it means simply that the group has a strong positive valence for them. This implies that the group exists cognitively for them, and it usually means that they will belong to it, although the possibility exists that someone can identify with a group that he does not belong to—for instance, because he lacks the prerequisites or sees the group as closed to him—just as someone can fail to identify with a group that he does belong to but believes he cannot leave. This way of thinking about the matter also points up the distinction between identification with one's own group and "prejudice" against out-groups: they are represented by separate vectors, and a positive valence for one need not imply a negative valence for another. Similarly, prejudice or hostility toward some group is an affective phenomenon, a valence; stereotyping should be regarded as a set of beliefs, as a purely cognitive phenomenon (although in common usage the word "stereotype" usually implies a negative valence).

In short, field theory seems to provide a useful way to sort things out, to make distinctions that we often fail to make, in order that the relationships among these phenomena can be examined empirically rather than simply being assumed. In the chapters that follow, we will look at these things one at a time, although not in this order and without the Lewinian terminology. This is not an attempt to "test a model" or even to build one in any rigorous sense but rather a preliminary exploration of this curious terrain. The flowers in this landscape may reflect the lack of attention that went into their cultivation, and they seem to be linked by a maze of paths, with a great many switchbacks and probably some dead ends. But there are some interesting specimens in here (and there is nothing wrong with dead ends, if the scenery is enjoyable). We can stroll down some of these causal paths, and speculate about where others might lead.

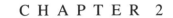

"Who Am I?"

Regional Affiliation

"Southernness" does not have to be viewed as a social-psycho-logical property at all. For some purposes, what is important is where somebody lives. Here, though, I am interested in South-erners not as an aggregate defined by residence in a particular piece of geography, but as a reference group, a cognitive entity that people use to orient themselves.[1] The correspondence be-tween these two ways of defining Southerners will obviously be close, but less than perfect. Some who have taken up temporary or even permanent residence outside the South still consider themselves Southerners and are so considered by their neighbors. Some who live in the South insist on their non-Southernness, even unto two or three generations, and others—willing enough to be Southerners—will not be allowed to forget their origins.

These two aspects of identity, self-designation and designation by others, are clearly more appropriate measures of Southern-ness, in the sense that concerns us here, than the simple datum, place of residence. With survey data, it is difficult to measure reliably how our respondents are viewed by others, but it is easy to find out how people view themselves. We told our respondents

1. See Hyman and Singer, *Readings in Reference Group Theory and Research.*

that "some people around here think of themselves as Southerners, others do not," then asked them: "How about you—would
you say that you are a Southerner or not?"

Although there is considerable variation in how much regional
consciousness our respondents display (that is, in how salient regional categories are to them), nearly all had enough to be able to
answer the question. Given the inevitably close association between residence and self-definition, perhaps it is no surprise that
82 percent of the nine hundred white North Carolinians who
answered this question said that they did regard themselves as
Southerners. Thirteen percent said they did not, and only the
remaining 5 percent said they were uncertain. When we urged
them to choose, a majority of this 5 percent said they were Southerners too.[2]

The Effects of Residential History

These responses, which indicate the presence or absence of what
might be called "regional affiliation," are crucial: from one point
of view, they define the population—Southerners—that we are
interested in. One might well ask what determines the answers we
received: birth? ancestry? "correct" racial views or religious affiliation? The answer, for the vast majority of our respondents, is
rather dull. Finding, as we do, that most of the variation in self-
definition is explained by residential history is rather like finding
that people tend to define themselves as Polish-American if they
had Polish ancestors. Nevertheless, for the record, Table 2.1
shows that most white North Carolinians who were born and
raised in the South consider themselves Southerners, and most
born and raised outside the South do not. People with border state
backgrounds are, appropriately, intermediate. Whether one went
to school outside the South (a rough measure of early residential

2. A bit less expected, perhaps, was the fact that 73 percent of the black respondents indicated that they were Southerners. Blacks were not more likely than
whites to say that they were *not* Southerners, but were twice as likely to say that
they did not know or were uncertain (see Appendix B).

Table 2.1. Percentage of Respondents Who Consider Themselves Southerners, by Birthplace and Place of Schooling

Birthplace	School attendance outside South (N)	
	Yes	No
South	87%	89%
	(54)	(723)
Border states	42%	73%
	(12)	(11)
Other states	29%	67%
	(70)	(6)

NOTE: Other responses are "not a Southerner" and "unsure, don't know." Eight foreign-born respondents are excluded from the table. Note that *any* non-Southern schooling should produce a "yes" response.

history) also affects responses to this question. Only 29 percent of those seventy respondents who were born outside the South and had at least some non-Southern schooling said they thought of themselves as Southerners. More refined measures of residential history would almost certainly explain a good deal of the remaining variation.[3]

Is that all there is to it? Are birthplace and residence the only things that matter? When we asked people why they had answered as they did, nearly 80 percent mentioned residence, and some of the responses reflected puzzlement that the answer was not obvious. Many said in so many words that the label was "just geographical," while others told us one way or another that they

3. And a better sample would let us answer another important question: I have suggested elsewhere that the best way to define "the South" is by looking at what proportion of the residents of different areas consider themselves to be Southerners. See Reed, *The Enduring South*, pp. 12–13, and Reed, *One South*, chap. 4, "The Heart of Dixie: An Essay in Folk Geography."

thought of themselves as Southerners just because (as one put it) "it's an accepted thing":

> A twenty-four-year-old mechanic:
> "I guess it's because I've always been told—brought up that way, I guess."

> A twenty-nine-year-old part-time legal secretary, wife of a corporation executive:
> "The environment—most everyone around here feels they are Southerners, and so I guess I do, too."

> A twenty-two-year-old university research technician, female:
> "It would be just a geographical thing. I think I could get along just as well if I lived in the North or West or anyplace else."

> A thirty-year-old university teaching assistant, divorced mother:
> "Because of the social stratosphere [sic] I was raised in—not because I feel great pride but because I'm aware of my environment."

> A fifty-five-year-old wife of a railway worker:
> "The reason I feel that way is that's all I know. I don't know any different than the South."

But over 20 percent of our respondents mentioned something other than residential history and geographical convention, and almost as many again mentioned residence *and* something else. For quite a few, regional affiliation was not simply a matter of where someone comes from, a conclusion indicated also by the fact that 44 percent of the respondents disagreed with the proposition that "people who move to the South from the North never really become Southerners" (with another 15 percent unsure).[4]

---

4. We shall encounter this statement again, as a measure of "regional prejudice," in chap. 6. As might be expected, among migrants to the South disagreement with this statement is almost a prerequisite for asserting that one is a Southerner oneself.

More than half of our respondents, it appears, believe that the regional group's boundaries are permeable: birthplace is not destiny, and Yankees can overcome their backgrounds if they try.

Other Determinants

Aside from residential history, the most common reason given for thinking of oneself as a Southerner is affection for other Southerners, a feeling of closeness to them and their ways—in other words, a sense of identification with the regional group. Nearly a quarter of the self-designated Southerners (a majority of those who mentioned something other than residence) gave reasons like these:

"I like [Southern] customs and habits."

"Southern people are good people."

"I have strong feelings toward the Southern tradition."

"I get along better here."

"I was raised with 'em [Southerners]."

"I identify with them."

Another frequent theme, accounting for most of the rest of the responses, had to do with the importance of *non-Southerners* for Southerners' self-definition. Some respondents indicated that they thought of themselves as Southerners because they had come to see that Southerners, themselves included, were different from Northerners:

A disabled female head of household:
"I know I'm not like a Yankee—that's about all."

A fifty-seven-year-old pharmacist:
"I went to school with people from the North and there are a lot of differences in the two."

An owner-manager of a garden service business:

"I'm different from Northerners—ways of talking, doing things, and thinking."

A twenty-three-year-old mother, Roman Catholic, typist:
"I've lived in the North and just feel I have more in common with Southerners."

A forty-four-year-old wife of a furniture worker:
"People away from here—I can't understand them. They talk funny."

A sixty-one-year-old housewife:
"We are not Northerners."

Others, perhaps 3 percent of those who thought of themselves as Southerners, added a note of hostility or dislike to their perceptions of regional differences. They thought of themselves as Southerners less because they liked other Southerners than because they disliked Northerners or the North:

A fifty-four-year-old contractor:
"I don't like these people from the North and I don't think like them."

A thirty-five-year-old father, bank collector:
"I used to drive a truck and go up north. People don't speak—[they're] self-centered. Southerners are friendly and help other people but don't interfere."

A twenty-two-year-old bachelor, college student, and maintenance worker for an apartment complex:
"When I was a kid I hated Yankees. Nothing will make you feel more like a Southerner than being around Yankees."

A forty-five-year-old wife of a credit manager:
"I . . . like Southerners. I don't get along too well with Northerners."

A thirty-three-year-old wife of a wholesale district manager for a national corporation:

"I . . . dislike some Northerners. (I don't think we think about this as much as we used to.)"

A thirty-year-old shipping department worker:
"I believe in the South. I'm just a Southern boy! I've been up north and I didn't like it. People are more friendly [here]. It's a better place to live."

A thirty-two-year-old wife of an architect:
"I lived up north and hated it. I just like it here."

A forty-four-year-old mechanic:
"I lived in the North and didn't like it."

A thirty-four-year-old typesetter, lives with her parents:
"I've been in New York and I like the South better. I don't like the big cities in the North. I like the people, but not the cities."

A thirty-seven-year-old father, assistant production supervisor in a factory:
"I don't like the way people in the North live."

Other respondents said they thought of themselves as Southerners because of the way that non-Southerners viewed them:

A twenty-three-year-old bookkeeper-secretary, separated from husband:
"Maybe because I was in Germany a couple of years and everybody told me I was a true Southerner."

A fifty-one-year-old textile machine operator, wife of a union organizer:
"We're treated as Southerners."

A thirty-five-year-old product manager, father:
"I have a Southern accent and people look on me as a Southerner."

A twenty-eight-year-old housewife:

"When I went to college I got this feeling from the people I met who were definitely Northern."

Finally, some respondents indicated that their sense of themselves as Southerners came out of the experience of being mistreated because of it, either as individual Southerners or as members of a regional group that is collectively abused in one way or another:

A twenty-two-year-old truck driver and handyman:
"Southern people get along with one another. They don't mock you like Northerners."

A forty-eight-year-old self-employed lumber worker:
"I've been talked at. When you get to New York, you look back and consider yourself a Southerner."

A "fortyish" nurse:
"I'm of the opinion that [Southerners] are not getting a fair shake politically. They're looked down on for no reason."

A seventy-three-year-old housewife:
"Because of the partiality shown on integration by the Supreme Court. I feel like we all ought to band together as Southerners. Northerners think they're better than we are. I didn't use to think of myself as a Southerner, but now I do."

A thirty-five-year-old textile mill worker, female:
"If anyone asks me I'll tell them I'm a Southerner. I feel that Southerners have had it worse than the others."

A forty-three-year-old attorney:
"Because [I] feel a resentment against busing and the tyranny which I feel busing represents."

A sixty-seven-year-old retired salesman:
"I think the North is still fighting the War between the States. The Northerners think that Southerners are lazy. The Northerners have had more advantages from the federal government until Franklin Roosevelt was elected."

There was a scattering of miscellaneous and idiosyncratic responses. (One man, echoing Brother Dave Gardner, told us he thought of himself as a Southerner because "I don't believe there is a North. The earth is a Southern planet.") For the most part, though, those who saw anything other than residence as relevant mentioned this sense of identification, whether it was based on affection for other Southerners, similarity to them, dislike of Northerners or the North itself, others' labeling of oneself, or a sense of grievance based on group membership. We shall come back to all of these themes in later chapters. For now, it is sufficient to note that they influence many people's responses, even to the basic question, "Would you say that you are a Southerner, or not?"

"Assimilated" Non-Southerners

A particularly interesting group for studying the effects of factors other than residence is that composed of people born and raised outside the South who have nevertheless come to think of themselves as Southerners. Most never do, as we saw in Table 2.1, and for those who do claim to be Southerners, there may be some question of the extent to which that claim is accepted. As we saw, many Southerners doubt that migrants can ever become Southerners.

Still, about a third of the migrants in our sample regard themselves as Southerners, and their reasons for doing so can be sorted into two broad, familiar categories. For a large minority, residence, however brief, is the defining criterion. Perhaps it is not surprising when a forty-five-year-old Marine officer from Pennsylvania says he is a Southerner because "I've lived here for fifteen years." But when a thirty-four-year-old man says he thinks of himself as a Southerner because "This is our adopted home. This is where we live," the fact that he moved from the Midwest only three years ago must be less important than the fact that he evidently intends to stay. Others who mentioned that they now live in the South added that they have married into it. A young manager, who emigrated from Germany eight years before we interviewed him, told us that "I've lived in the South as long as I've been in the U. S.," and added: "My wife's family are true Southerners." A retired Marine, a native New Yorker, told us he had lived in the South for thirty years and had also "married a Southern gal."

As might be expected, however, these assimilated migrants are less likely than native Southerners to base their affiliation on their residential histories. For them, it is much more a matter of choice, and most have based that choice on a sense of identification with regional group, usually because they feel an affinity for the people of the South and find them or some of their traits admirable. A few examples will give the flavor of these responses:

> "Southerners are sincere and lovable," said a retired businessman, who had moved from the Midwest twenty-five years before. "We feel much more at home here."

> A fifty-year-old chemical engineer, who had moved from New York about the same time, said he lived in the South "by choice." He felt "a kinship" with Southerners. In particular, he said, "I'm in no big hurry."

> A Roman Catholic management analyst, who spent three months at Parris Island during World War II, brought his family back after the war because "I like it here—the climate and the people."

> The middle-aged wife of a bank clerk, who had moved from California twenty years earlier, said, "I've lived all over, but I like it here the best. I just feel closer to people in the South." (Her husband, she added, is "a native Southerner.")

> A thirty-five-year-old housewife and mother, married to a chemical plant manager, had lived in North Carolina ten years. She thought of herself as a Southerner, she said, because "I like the slow pace. Also the friendliness. It's just my home and I like it."

A thirty-four-year-old accountant, father of two children, said he had moved from New York and become a Southerner because "I approve of [Southerners'] general attitude on raising children and respect." Also, he added, "I am a States' Righter."

Finally, a sixty-one-year-old worker in an electrical parts plant, who had come from Pennsylvania eighteen years earlier, told us that "I made up my mind before I came down here that I would be one of the best rebels they ever had. Southern people are good people. They are more neighborly. I come from the North and I should know."

In one case we had a response that may be more significant than its rarity might indicate. A forty-eight-year-old native of Pennsylvania who had lived in the South for twenty-six years told us that he was a Southerner because "I'm living here and have to do things the way their life is." He did not sound very happy about it; for him, Southernness may have had an element of protective coloration.

In any case, non-Southern migrants who have come to regard themselves as Southerners give the same sorts of reasons for holding this self-concept that natives do, but they are more likely to view affiliation as a matter of choice and more likely to have given some thought to what it is that makes someone "a Southerner." This self-consciousness, as we shall see, is characteristic of people who are somehow marginal to the regional group.

"Lapsed" Southerners

Of course, many who were born and raised in the South also see Southernness as something one can accept or reject, and a few of them have exercised that choice to come up with a self-definition that would not have been predicted from their residential histories. Seven percent of the North Carolinians we interviewed who

were born in the South and grew up there said that they did not
regard themselves as Southerners. When we asked them why not,
most gave answers that indicated a lack of identification with the
group: a few said forthrightly that they did not like Southerners;
more said that they possessed "un-Southern" attitudes or characteristics that somehow disqualified them. One young, male,
elementary-school teacher said he did not think of himself as a
Southerner because he did not like the company it would put him
in. "I never cared to associate with them [Southerners]. We don't
think the same." (Bear in mind that this man was born and raised
in the South and now teaches in North Carolina.) Many other
respondents told us they were not Southerners because they did
not "think the same." Some seemed to agree with the historian
Ulrich B. Phillips that "the cardinal test of a Southerner" is devo-
tion to white supremacy: lacking this, they felt that they did not
want to be, or could not be regarded as, Southerners.[5] A young
laborer, working for a nurseryman, told our interviewer: "A lot of
Southerners are against the Negroes. I don't got anything against
them." The thirty-two-year-old wife of a real estate salesman said
much the same thing: "I don't feel as strong as Southerners I have
heard speak do on the racial issue. I'm not that much one way."
Also, she added, "I don't dislike Northerners," suggesting another implicit criterion.

Only a few of our respondents, however, located themselves
outside the group (or inside it, for that matter) solely on the basis
of their racial views, which seems to bear out the findings of other
studies that racial ideology is no longer, if it ever was, a shib-
boleth for Southern affiliation.[6] Rather more common was dis-
affiliation based on more general political or cultural disagreement with "Southern attitudes," which may, of course, include
racial attitudes as a component. The psychological émigrés who
gave this sort of response were almost always young, well-
educated, middle-class individuals who *did* often differ strikingly
from those around them. One college student (born and raised in

5. Phillips, "The Central Theme of Southern History."
6. See Reed, *One South*, chap. 5, "The Cardinal Test of a Southerner?"

the South but an agnostic and a liberal Democrat) said he did not think of himself as a Southerner because "I'm not the typical Southerner—too liberal." Similarly, a thirtyish small business-man, who told us he really wanted to be a schoolteacher, said he was not a Southerner because "I don't agree with Southern politi-cal attitudes"; a young salesman said he was not because "I'm a liberal person"; and an engineer's wife—a young mother, part-time student, and Unitarian—said she was not because "so often my viewpoint isn't the same as the typical Southerner."

A very few respondents mentioned more idiosyncratic factors that set them apart from Southerners. A middle-aged drugstore cashier, for instance, said that she did not "talk like a South-erner," referring to her accent, which our interviewer agreed was only "slightly Southern." But these, too, were operating with a mental image of Southerners that implied something more than residence in the South; they believed that they were too different to be, or to be allowed to be, part of the group. With our data, it is impossible to say whether most of these people feel that their "un-Southern" characteristics *disqualify* them or whether they simply do not "care to associate" themselves with Southerners: It is diffi-cult to say, in other words, who is rejecting whom.

However, for another large group of lifelong Southern residents who do not think of themselves as Southerners, it is very clear who is doing the rejecting: they are, on ideological grounds that have been around since the Civil War. These people feel that being Southern was "un-American" in 1860 and still is. When we asked why they said they were not Southerners, they told us, for exam-ple, "It's not where you're from but how you feel. I'm an Ameri-can." (The man who said that was a forty-three-year-old in-surance salesman, a Wallace supporter, and a segregationist.) Several respondents said simply, "I'm just an American." A middle-aged widow said, "I don't section myself. I'm just all-American." A retired mother argued, "An American is the impor-tant thing. One nation as a whole." A middle-aged truck driver said, "I consider myself an American. It's one country and every-one is a citizen of it." A twenty-year-old cloth-cutter in a furniture factory told us, "I'm an American. The Civil War is past."

Those who dissociate themselves from Southerners on essentially Unionist grounds come from all age groups, all social classes, and both sexes, but they come disproportionately from mountain and hill areas in western and north central North Carolina, areas of strong Union sentiment during the Civil War.[7] It looks very much as if the Civil War is *not* past within some family traditions or in some communities in the South.[8]

Roughly two-thirds of the respondents who were born and brought up in the South but did not think of themselves as Southerners rejected that label on either ideological or perceptual grounds: they did not want to be Southerners or felt they were too different from the "typical Southerner" to qualify. The remaining third were not so much unwilling to regard themselves as Southerners as *unable* to do so: the concept was not one they understood. These respondents, approximately 2 percent of the total white sample, lacked not only regional identification but regional consciousness. Although they told us they were not Southerners, they resembled some of the respondents who could not tell us whether they were or were not, because they did not understand the question.[9] When we asked these people why they did not regard themselves as Southerners, some of them told us they could not say, but others were more helpful. "I don't know what it [Southerner] means," a retired farmer told us. "Don't think too much [about] the South," said a seventy-two-year-old widow.

7. Specifically, in this sample, they come from Stokes and Avery counties, which supplied nearly a quarter of *all* respondents born and raised in the South who did not think of themselves as Southerners.

8. And not just in the South. On the persistence of regional attitudes formed a century ago, see Reed, *The Enduring South*, pp. 17–18, which show that anti-Southern attitudes outside the South are most commonly found in New England, and there (further analysis of the data shows) among Republicans.

9. In Lewinian terms, the concept "Southerners" does not exist in the cognitive space of these respondents, or it is so poorly defined that they cannot say whether it includes them or not. This is clearly a different situation from that of someone who has a representation of the group but sees himself as marginal to it or outside it altogether. Our interviewers commented: "R[espondent] thought a lot of questions were crazy, did not seem to have thought much, feel she was genuinely ignorant"; "R[espondent] didn't understand South and Southerners"; and the like.

Three respondents evidently believed that living in the South had something to do with it but were uncertain about whether North Carolina was in the South (one asked her husband).

Nearly all of those who had difficulty understanding the concept "Southerner" were very elderly individuals or poorly educated females—the usual types of people that make up what survey researchers have called "chronic know-nothings." [10] For a few, however, the cognitive impoverishment may have been temporary: one retired hard-rock miner was drinking moonshine during the interview, a fact, our interviewer noted cautiously, that "may have influenced responses."

If there are some people to whom the concept "Southerner" is simply meaningless, or almost so, because they seldom have occasion to use it, there are a few others who have used it and concluded that the category is not a useful one. A twenty-three-year-old sheet metal worker told us he was not a Southerner, despite having been born in the South and raised there; when we asked why not, he said: "When I was in the service, I was in with people from the North, the West, and all over. They all seemed alike to me." Similarly, a former short-order cook, retired at forty with a disability, told us she had lived other places: "It doesn't make any difference."

Some people, in other words, have no mental construct corresponding to the word "Southerner" because they have never learned one and never needed one. Others may once have had one, but have come to believe that the distinction makes no difference. This latter group is small (only a handful of our respondents fall into it) but noteworthy because here a lack of regional consciousness reflects not isolation and lack of experience with non-Southerners, but rather the opposite. This general idea—that some people do not know enough to think in regional terms, while a few feel they know too much to do so—will be confirmed in the next chapter, when we turn to an examination of the effects of interregional experience on regional stereotyping.

10. Hyman and Sheatsley, "Some Reasons Why Information Campaigns Fail."

Affiliation, Consciousness, and Identification

It appears, then, that regional affiliation, declaring that one is or is not a Southerner, is intimately and necessarily related to both regional consciousness and regional identification. Although residential history plays a major role in determining regional affiliation (analogous to that of ancestry in determining ethnic affiliation), other factors can and do enter in, particularly for those people who are objectively marginal to the regional group, those who are likely to feel that they have a choice in the matter. These people are likely to base their choice on a sense of identification (or lack of it) with other members of the group, and they are likely as well to have thought about Southernness, to exhibit relatively high levels of regional consciousness. There are also others who have difficulty choosing or who decide erratically, not because they are marginal between the regional group and the "outside world" but because they are marginal in the sense of being socially "out of it"—isolated by poverty, rurality, infirmity, stultifying sex roles, or lack of education. These people lack not only regional identification but its prerequisite, regional consciousness.

Of course, among those who simply acknowledge, more or less as a matter of fact, that they are Southerners, both consciousness and identification will vary. Some will not have given much thought to their regional affiliation; others will be highly self-conscious about it. Some will feel strongly bound to the South; others will not feel any particular ties; still others will regret the fact of their affiliation. From this analysis, we have some clues concerning the determinants of consciousness and identification. In the next two chapters, we shall examine them more directly.

CHAPTER 3

"What Is a Southerner?"

Regional Consciousness

We have seen that the question "Are you a Southerner?" can give people difficulty for two very different reasons. On the one hand, someone may have a perfectly adequate mental representation of the group but still not know whether it includes him, because he is genuinely a borderline case. His regional consciousness may be high but his location marginal. This is, in fact, a relatively frequent combination: as we shall see, marginality often *produces* high consciousness.

On the other hand, someone may have no cognitive representation of the category "Southerner," or one too vague and ill-defined for him to know who is and is not in the category. Presumably, most Americans do not know whether they live in amateur radio call-sign area four, indeed, do not know what amateur radio call-sign areas are. Few have any "call-sign area consciousness." Similarly, we saw some North Carolinians for whom the concepts "South" and "Southerner" had little or no meaning: the concepts were simply not part of their cognitive apparatus.

But I should emphasize again that most Americans and nearly all Southerners have some mental construction labeled "Southerner," some degree of regional consciousness. Only a small minority of our sample had difficulty telling us whether they were

Southerners, and only a minority of that minority had difficulty because they did not understand the question. Among those who displayed enough regional consciousness to answer the question, however, there was a considerable degree of variation in how *much* regional consciousness they possessed. At the other extreme from those for whom regional concepts have no meaning are people for whom the construct "Southerner" is very salient, people who often think in regional terms and for whom regional categories are an important way to divide up the world of their experience.

What background factors and experiences produce regional consciousness? How does someone come to hold a cognitive construct labeled "Southerner" and to believe it is useful? If certain conditions are met, this sort of "knowledge" can be obtained either first hand, through experience with other regional groups, or second hand, from others in one's family or community or from the mass media.[1] That is, one can learn that regional groups exist and something about their characteristics either by being told about them or by observing and generalizing on one's own.

To some extent, American regions and regional groups are cultural products, at large in American culture, part of its folklore. Like other culturally given distinctions, this one is learned more or less unthinkingly as one grows into that culture. Regional concepts are part of the vocabulary of the national discourse, and those who wish or are obliged to follow that discourse will acquire the vocabulary. Recall that those who were least likely to be able to think in these terms were people isolated from the national culture—by poverty, rurality, lack of education, and the like. We can surmise that high degrees of regional consciousness will be found among those most attuned to supralocal culture, whether by education, exposure to the mass media, or living and working in a relatively cosmopolitan setting. It is not merely that such people are more likely to think in terms of generalizations and abstrac-

1. This distinction corresponds to that between "non-normative" and "normative" stereotypes proposed by Triandis in "Frequency of Contact and Stereotyping," if the invidious connotations of the word "stereotype" are disregarded.

tions in the first place, although certainly education, in particular, is often supposed to have that effect. It is, rather, that such people are more likely to have come into contact with regional concepts, to have found them useful, and to have had them "stick."[2]

Determinants of Regional Consciousness

An index of regional consciousness will help us to explore these ideas. We asked respondents who said they thought of themselves as Southerners: "How often do you think of yourself as a Southerner? Very often, sometimes, or hardly at all?" At the end of the interview, to minimize "spillover," we returned to the subject: "How much thought would you say you have given to the South and to Southerners before today? Quite a lot, some, only a little, or almost none?" Each of these questions was scored zero, one, or two, according to how much regional consciousness the answer displayed, and the two scores were simply added to give an index score ranging from zero to four. Thirty-six percent of the white respondents who defined themselves as Southerners scored three or four, displaying high regional consciousness, if we take that to mean that they said they (1) often think of themselves as Southerners and had given at least some thought to the subject before the interview or (2) think of themselves as Southerners at least sometimes and had given quite a lot of thought to the subject in the past.

Table 3.1 shows how this index is related to a number of items that it seemingly *ought* to be related to. One's "interest in how [other group members] as a whole are getting along" has been used in the past as a measure of group identification, but it seems to have more to do with what we are calling "consciousness" here. Certainly it is strongly related to our index: 81 percent of those with high scores on the index indicated a good deal of interest, compared to only 36 percent of those with the lowest score.

2. In *The Enduring Effects of Education*, Hyman, Wright, and Reed show that this is the case for concepts and "knowledge" of many different sorts.

Table 3.1. Relation of Consciousness Index to Measures of Attention to Regional Matters

	Consciousness Index				
	Low 0	1	2	3	High 4
Have "a good deal of interest in how Southerners as a whole are getting along"	36%	38%	48%	62%	81%
Do not know whether Northerners or Southerners are doing better economically	21%	17%	13%	11%	6%
Do not know whether Northerners "have more power in Washington than is fair"	35%	29%	22%	14%	10%
Have "a great deal of interest" in Southern history	10%	17%	27%	38%	58%
Agree that the Southern way of life is different (other responses are "no difference" and "don't know")	48%	50%	53%	66%	75%
(N)	(78)	(186)	(180)	(148)	(129)

Scores on the index are also related to "don't know" responses to questions about regional economic and political comparisons: not surprisingly, people who do not think much in regional terms are unlikely to have thought about these matters enough to have even an incorrect conclusion. An interest in the South's history (a subject we shall return to later) is also related to our measure of consciousness, as is the conclusion that the South has a different way of life from the rest of the country. This last association may be less straightforward than it appears. Not only are those with little regional consciousness likely to say "don't know" when asked if the Southern way of life is different, it may be that those who are persuaded that there are no important regional differences display, in consequence, low levels of regional consciousness.

We saw in the last chapter some extreme cases of low regional consciousness: the background factors and experiences related to our index are in reasonably good accord with what we would expect, given the characteristics of those extreme cases (Table 3.2). Forty-six percent of the 82 college graduates in the sample, for instance, showed high regional consciousness, compared to 33 percent of the 336 respondents who did not complete high school. Similarly, those who live in cities, suburbs, and towns are more likely than rural folk to show high regional consciousness. Watching television news, reading newspapers, and visiting the public library are all related to regional consciousness, results consistent with a great deal of other research on the correlates of informed public opinion. Sex and income are only slightly related to regional consciousness, and the slight associations are almost certainly due to their associations with education. The same may be true for the modest and inconsistent pattern of association between consciousness and occupation.

Self-reported social-class membership is essentially unrelated to regional consciousness, but it is interesting that those who are unable or unwilling to assign themselves to a social class—who display low class consciousness, in other words—are also less likely than others to display high regional consciousness. This suggests that the willingness or ability to categorize oneself may be a generalized phenomenon. As the twenty-four-year-old wife of a farm laborer told us, when we asked why she did not think of herself as a Southerner, "I just don't think of myself as Southern or anything else in particular." Certainly there is no indication here that regional consciousness, as we have defined it, precludes class consciousness.

To summarize, Table 3.2 shows that regional consciousness is most acute among educated, urban, white-collar, well-informed respondents—among the types of Southerners one is increasingly likely to encounter. This may seem puzzling if the precise mean-

Table 3.2. Regional Consciousness, by Selected Background
Variables and Behaviors

	High Consciousness	(N)
Men	39%	(330)
Women	38%	(399)
Middle class (self-reported)	42%	(245)
Working class (self-reported)	41%	(326)
"Don't think in terms of classes"	29%	(158)
Income under $5,000	34%	(193)
Income between $5,000 and $10,000	39%	(250)
Income over $10,000	41%	(243)
Less than high school education	33%	(336)
High school graduate	42%	(311)
College graduate	46%	(82)
Urban or suburban residence	43%	(447)
Rural residence	32%	(282)
Professional or managerial workers	35%	(57)
Clerical or sales workers	42%	(180)
Skilled laborers and operatives	26%	(61)
Unskilled and service workers	37%	(145)
Farmers and farm laborers	46%	(13)
Watched television news day before	41%	(361)
Did not watch television news day before	36%	(366)
Read newspaper in last two days	40%	(553)
Did not read newspaper in last two days	33%	(175)
Went to library in past year	47%	(225)
Did not go to library in past year	35%	(503)

ing of "consciousness" is not kept in mind: here it means simply thinking about and in terms of regions. It is not a form of parochialism: on the contrary, since "region" is by its nature a *contrast* concept, emphasizing the distinction between the region and its surroundings, those who most often encounter the region's surroundings should be most likely to find regional concepts useful in dealing with their experience—assuming that the concepts are useful ones in the first place.

The Effects of Experience Outside the South

This brings us to the second way of developing or maintaining such concepts: not vicariously but directly, through experience and observation of one's own. Table 3.3 presents several indications that exposure to non-Southerners is a potent "consciousness-raising experience" for Southerners. The level of regional consciousness is substantially higher among Southerners who have lived outside the South than among those who have not.[3] A majority (50 percent) of those born outside the South show high consciousness, compared to 38 percent of the Southern-born. Thirty-seven percent of those who have never lived outside the South show high consciousness; 47 percent of those who have lived outside the region do so. Even traveling outside the South appears to have some effect: those who have traveled more than five hundred miles from home (which may include some who have never left the South) show higher levels of regional consciousness than those who have not, particularly those few respondents who have never been more than two hundred miles from their homes.

The effects of non-Southern schooling are similar (as might be expected, since the exposure variables are obviously related to one another) and are presented here only because of a suggestive

3. Here and elsewhere, when we speak of Southerners who have lived outside the South, we are dealing with those who have lived outside the South *and returned*. Obviously, those who remain outside the region may be different, and the possibility of self-selection cannot be ignored, although these data do not allow us to address it.

Table 3.3. Regional Consciousness, by Exposure to Non-South

	High Consciousness	(N)
Born in South	38%	(695)
Born in border states	38%	(8)
Born outside South	50%	(26)
No schooling outside South	37%	(660)
One year or less non-Southern schooling	63%	(30)
1–5 years non-Southern schooling	47%	(17)
6+ years non-Southern schooling	50%	(22)
No travel more than 200 miles away	9%	(23)
Travel 200–500 miles from home	29%	(114)
Travel 500 miles from home	42%	(585)
No residence outside South	37%	(630)
Residence outside South	47%	(99)

reversal at the extreme high end of the exposure continuum. Consciousness increases with education outside the South, but those with more than a year of it show a lower level of consciousness (although still a high one) than those with less than a year. The numbers of respondents involved are small, but this curvilinear pattern should remind us that some respondents who said they did not think in regional terms at all gave as their reason that experience had convinced them that regional distinctions were not useful. We shall encounter this curvilinear pattern again.

We can construct an index of extraregional exposure to summarize our respondents' experience outside the South. "Low Exposure" refers to those who were born in the South and have never left it (or, to be precise, have never been more than five hundred miles from home). "Traveled in North" refers to those Southern-born respondents who have never lived outside the South but who have traveled more than five hundred miles from home. "Lived in North" refers to all those who have done so except those with "Extensive Exposure," that is, born in the North or having gone to school there for a year or more.

Obviously, exposure is related to education, occupation, and the other variables examined in Table 3.2, but Table 3.4 suggests that the effects are independent. (When controlling for education, I have collapsed the categories "Lived in North" and "Extensive Exposure" to give adequate bases for percentaging.) At every level of education, those with higher levels of exposure show higher levels of consciousness, and at each level of exposure, education seems to produce at least a slight increase in consciousness (although the effects of exposure are stronger). The lowest level of regional consciousness is found among respondents who have never been outside the South and are not high school graduates: only 18 percent display high consciousness. It appears that education can substitute to some extent for firsthand experience,

Table 3.4. Regional Consciousness, by Exposure Index and Education

	Percentage with High Consciousness (N)			
Education	Low Exposure	Traveled in North	Lived in North	Extensive Exposure
All white Southern respondents	24% (140)	39% (456)	46% (59)	55% (74)
Not high school graduate	18% (92)	38% (211)	45% (33)	
High school graduate	36% (45)	40% (197)	52% (69)	
College graduate	* (3)	44% (48)	55% (31)	

*Base too small to compute reliable percentage.

serving perhaps as a sort of vicarious "exposure." College graduates who have only traveled in the North display about the same
level of regional consciousness as those who have lived in the
North but did not finish high school.

These findings should not come as a surprise to students of
ethnic and racial groups, who have seen analogous findings for
other groups. Among blacks, for instance, racial consciousness is
highest, not among lower-class blacks in all-black neighborhoods,
but among middle-class blacks whose occupations and housing
patterns place them in frequent contact with whites. In an all-
black situation, race is not salient, just as region is seldom salient
for Southerners who never leave the South, nor water, ordinarily,
for fish.[4]

Exposure to non-Southerners can raise the regional consciousness of Southerners in two rather different ways. In the first place,
as the feminist movement has reminded us, being treated as a
member of a category rather than as an individual can heighten
one's awareness of the category and the process of categorization.
Realizing that one's sex, race, ethnic group, or regional origin is
salient to others, that it structures at least their initial responses to
oneself, can certainly produce *self*-consciousness about attributes
that may not previously have been considered very important. It
is not necessary to explicate Charles Horton Cooley's concept of
the "looking-glass self" to realize that we see ourselves in large
measure as others see us, or as we believe others see us. Relations
across group boundaries are socially important in part because
they reinforce those very boundaries by reminding the participants that the groups exist and that they are members of them.[5]

4. A typical finding was that reported by Rosenberg and Simmons in *Black and
White Self-Esteem*, where they compared black schoolchildren in all-black schools
to those in mixed schools. Rosenberg has also written of the effects of interaction
across religious lines, in "The Dissonant Religious Context and Emotional Disturbance." When the interaction is conflict-laden, the effects on group consciousness
are particularly marked: see, for instance, Vallee, "Regionalism and Ethnicity."
5. This point has been made, in different ways, by theorists as diverse as Georg
Simmel, George Herbert Mead, and Jean Piaget. As Gouldner and Peterson put it in
Notes on Technology and the Moral Order, "The self grows in self-consciousness
when it does not view itself exactly as others do" (p. 43).

It is not necessary that the categorical treatment be invidious, that it be what we usually call "discrimination" (although that probably helps), merely that it be categorical. Although there is evidence of occasional discrimination against Southerners (some time back, for instance, it was revealed that those with Southern accents were barred from some Congressional staff appointments), most Southerners can also attest to the fact that some non-Southerners have extremely flattering views of them. That is not the point. Whether one is admired or despised, favored or mistreated, is less important in the generation of group consciousness than the fact that the different treatment is based on group membership. Sociologists have written of "fraternal deprivation," rather less of "fraternal advantage," but in either case the realization that what one gets depends on membership in some category can heighten one's awareness that the category exists.[6]

One frequent example—innocuous and neutral, on the face of it—is what might be called the "spokesman phenomenon." The question "What do you people think about . . . ?" and its variants imply that the questioner sees "you people" as a socially significant group and his respondent as a representative member. In some ways the form of the question is more telling than its content, or the nature of an accurate answer. No one would ask such a question with "you people" referring to left-handers, but if people did so often enough, we would certainly begin to see more self-conscious southpaws.[7]

Lewis Killian tells a story that is very much to the point. When he first took a position at a New England university, he found himself in a receiving line for new faculty. The president of the university exchanged conventional pleasantries with several for-

6. See Vanneman and Pettigrew, "Race and Relative Deprivation in the Urban United States"; Runciman, *Relative Deprivation and Social Justice*; and, especially, Blumer, "Race Prejudice as a Sense of Group Position."

7. See Royce's discussion of the related topic of "tokens," in *Ethnic Identity*, p. 200. "Tokens cannot escape notice, being viewed as symbols of their category. . . . Tokens are expected to behave in accordance with the stereotypes of their category held by the dominants." Royce makes the extremely interesting observation that tokens function to "reinforce the sense of shared values among dominants," but only when they behave stereotypically.

eign visitors ahead of Killian in the line, but, hearing Killian's accent, asked *him* if he longed for home. At that point, he says, he did.[8]

In short, exposure to non-Southerners can heighten Southerners' regional consciousness through a reactive process. Southerners can observe that non-Southerners use regional concepts to structure *their* experience. There is good evidence to show that regional stereotypes are widespread in the United States, and Southerners who have occasion to deal with non-Southerners are more likely than those who do not to find themselves on the receiving end of such preconceptions.

The Nature of Regional Stereotypes

But regional consciousness is not related just to *others'* stereotypes. The other way in which interaction with non-Southerners can raise the regional consciousness of Southerners is by exposing them to regional differences and leading them to generalize about those differences: in other words, by generating regional stereotypes in Southerners. Those with high regional consciousness, we saw, are more likely than others to believe that "the Southern way of life" actually is different from that elsewhere in the United States. We can call their beliefs about that difference their "stereotypes," if we define the term carefully.

By stereotype, I mean here simply someone's cognitive representation of a group or category ("image" would be as good a word), a type of generalization that is virtually prerequisite for thinking about a group at all.[9] Someone with high regional con-

8. Peter Rose relates this story in his foreword to Killian's book, *White Southerners*, p. x. Other anecdotal support for this and many points I am making here can be found in Lisa Alther's novel, *Original Sins*. Many of her vignettes, I happen to know, are based on fact.

9. This is the sense in which Walter Lippmann first used the word in a psychological context, in *Public Opinion* (1922). Someone's stereotype of a social category may be more or less "derogatory" (as judged by some observer), associated with either positive or negative evaluation or "affect," idiosyncratic or widely

sciousness is, by definition, someone who thinks about regions and regional groups: presumably that thought has some content and such a person therefore holds regional stereotypes of some sort. The survey material offers some-evidence suggesting that most of our respondents do indeed see the South as different from the rest of the United States and Southerners as different from other Americans, and that there is a good deal of agreement on what the important differences are.[10]

Although some complained about heat, humidity, insects, and the like when asked for "the worst thing about the South," most respondents seemed to like the physical environment of their region. When we asked what the *best* thing is, two-thirds mentioned the South's climate, its forests, mountains, or coast, its lack of crowding and pollution, the opportunities it offers for outdoor recreation. In general, they seemed to agree with William Faulkner's view that the South is fortunate that God has done so much for it, and man so little:

> "[I like] the open spaces, the uncrowded roads and countryside. The physical environment agrees with me."-

> "The climate, the mild winter and change of seasons; the fact that air pollution and overcrowding isn't as prevalent as in the Northeast."

> "It's green, clean looking, not eat-up with pollution."

---

shared, more or less differentiated, and more or less accurate (although we can assume that no stereotype will do full justice to reality).

10. This evidence comes primarily from the verbatim answers to these questions: (1) What is the most important difference between the South and the rest of the country? (2) What would you say is the best thing about the South? and (3) What would you say is the worst thing about the South? Although the last two questions did not add "compared to the North," many respondents evidently heard it that way. Responses to the "best thing" question, for example, included one of "Everything is better than the North" and another of "I wouldn't say it's any better place than the North." The "most important difference" often turned up again as the "best thing" or the "worst thing," so I have here simply combined responses to the three questions to let our respondents say in their own words what they see as important regional differences.

"I like the climate and open spaces and the fresh food."

"It's beautiful here. A good place to bring children up. Living conditions are better in general. Recreation is better. I like to fish."

"I like the mountains, beaches. . . . This is just a good place to live. Not as crowded or polluted as the North."

"Used to be able to say clean air, but you can't say that any more. There's plenty of room to stretch out."

This last theme—"room to stretch out"—was echoed by a number of respondents, who volunteered that the South is "not as crowded" as the North, that it still offers "roominess" and "wide open spaces," that people are "not piled up so bad." Several mentioned "freedom" in the same breath as lack of crowding. Coupled with this claustrophobia was appreciation of the absence of cities and city problems, in particular environmental and social pollution. Only one respondent even implied that city lights had any attraction: the most important difference between South and North, she said rather wistfully, is that there is "more drinking and social life up there."

Unlike the South's attractions, its disadvantages are mostly man-made. Although a substantial minority (about one in five) responded to the question concerning the worst thing about the South by saying that there is *nothing* bad about it, the most frequent response to that question mentioned aspects of Southern society—its race relations, politics, or economy. There were more than occasional references to "backward" government or laws (including "the tax on Coca-Colas"), to racial integration or the lack of it, to poor schools, roads, or public transportation. Far and away the most frequent complaint, however, was economic. As one respondent put it, "I can't think of anything bad about it [the South], other than we don't make too much money down here." Many respondents mentioned low wages as the worst thing about the South, and a few brought it up as the "most important difference" between South and North. In many cases, it seems, they had their own wages in mind, as did the housewife who said the worst thing about the South is "low wages, absolutely. I could do more if my husband could make more money." Others saw the problem in less personal terms, saying that the worst thing about the South is the absence of the tax base necessary for better public services (e.g., "not having enough money to build more and better schools") or the effects of poverty on the poor (e.g., "[the worst thing is] poverty—ignorance and the great malnutrition among the very poor").

But our respondents clearly have images not just of the South but of *Southerners*. In other words, they have regional stereotypes. When we asked for the best thing about the South we did not limit respondents to one answer, and half volunteered that the best thing about the South is its people. The question about the most important difference between South and North produced even more responses that referred to the character and culture of Southerners (and a handful of respondents mentioned Southerners when asked to indicate the worst thing about the South).

Southerners are, by their own reckoning, slower, more traditional, and more polite and friendly than other Americans—a constellation of traits that, as some studies have shown, other Americans are generally prepared to grant them.[11]

Some mentioned the South's "slower pace" with approval:

"[Southerners are] not in such a run all the time—not so much hurry. People will talk to you."

"[The most important difference is] the pace of living."

"We don't push like they do."

"Everything not being so hectic."

"A less frantic tempo—a greater sense of belonging."

"Not so much pressure or anxiety—high pace—overall."

A few shared much the same perception but evidently had their doubts about whether the comparison was to the South's advantage:

11. Reed, *The Enduring South*, pp. 24–26.

"[The worst thing about the South is] lack of ambition.
We're all lazy."

"[The most important difference is] slower and poorer
people."

The same ambivalence was evident in comments on Southern
conservatism or traditionalism, which was mentioned by some
respondents as the best thing about the South, by others as the
worst. Southerners, some told us, are "too slow to change,"
"narrow-minded," or "a little backward in [their] thinking." Others approved of Southern religiosity, the strength of family ties,
and other values that might fairly be viewed as conservative.
"The kids from up north learn to be destructive and are messed
up," was one man's assessment, while another said the best thing
about the South is that "we don't have hippies."

Far and away the most frequent characterization of Southerners
(by these Southerners) was an elaboration on the theme that
Southerners are *good people*, as several said in so many words.
"Good," to our respondents, meant primarily pleasant to be
around: "considerate," "friendly," "hospitable," "polite," "gen-
tle," "gracious," "cordial," "genteel," "courteous," "congenial," "nice"—all of these our respondents' words, many of
them used often. Dissenting opinions were rare and were almost
entirely voiced by migrants from the North. One said the worst
thing about the South is "the attitude of Southerners . . . especially if you're from New York state." Another: "They are so
hostile about some things." However, some migrants felt the same
as natives ("They've been very nice to me"), and most Southerners were unstinting in their praise of each other:

> "People in the South for the most part are more cordial and
> courteous than those I've found in the North. People have
> more consideration of one another."

> "It's a sort of graciousness—gentility and a hospitality feel-
> ing—in people native to the South."

> "Well, I find people friendly here everywhere I go."

"There are some good people around."

"There is more communication between the people of the South."

"I have a great feeling of being respected and welcomed here."

"[The best thing about the South is] the attitude and friendly people as a whole. We live more like God intended us to live in relation to one another."

Learning about Regional Differences

At this point, we will make a distinction that may look somewhat artificial at first. To the extent that these warm feelings and this high regard indicate *identification* with one's fellow Southerners, we will examine the causes and consequences of that identification in the next chapter. To the extent that these feelings represent attempts to generalize about actual regional differences in attitudes and behavior, they tell us something about the content of Southerners' regional *stereotypes*; and that subject concerns us here.

Not all of our respondents shared the conventional view of what differentiates Southerners from other Americans, and some had no idea at all. Where do these views come from? What kinds of background and experience produce these perceptions? Certainly they are learned somehow, and one possibility suggested by the analysis of the antecedents of regional consciousness is that they are learned through exposure to non-Southerners. Such exposure increases the regional consciousness of Southerners. Does it also increase their readiness to generalize about the differences between non-Southerners and themselves in conventional ways? If there are cultural differences between Southerners and other Americans (and a substantial body of literature indicates that there certainly are), is it possible that the effect of interregional interaction is to produce stereotypes where none existed before or to strengthen existing ones (to the extent that they are accurate)?[12]

It appears that it is possible. We constructed an index of stereotyping from adjectives presented to respondents as follows: "Now I'm going to read some words that people use to describe other people. I'm going to ask you whether each word applies more to Northerners or to Southerners. Do you think ____ applies more to Northerners or to Southerners?" The ten adjectives were chosen on the basis of pretesting that showed widespread perceptions of regional differences in those respects. "Courteous," "religious," "patriotic," "slow," "generous," and "loyal to family" are often seen as Southern traits, their opposites being, by implication at least, Northern traits. "Aggressive," "industrious," "materialistic," and "sophisticated" are traits likely to be ascribed by Southerners to Northerners.[13]

12. This discussion owes much to Triandis, "Frequency of Contact and Stereotyping." See Reed, *One South*, chap. 6, "Getting to Know You," for a fuller treatment, which attempts to reconcile this line of thought with the long-lived research tradition in social psychology on the "contact hypothesis," namely, that intergroup interaction reduces "prejudice," a term often construed to include, if not to mean, stereotyping. On regional stereotypes, see also Gould and White, *Mental Maps*. A recent symposium edited by David L. Hamilton, *Cognitive Processes in Stereotyping and Intergroup Behavior*, addresses many of these issues and demonstrates that research and theory in this area have been revitalized (largely, it appears, because of renewed interest in the study of sex-role stereotypes). Henri Tajfel's article, "Social Stereotypes and Social Groups," in Turner and Giles, *Intergroup Behavior*, contains an intelligent discussion that reports some recent European research on the subject. For evidence that regional differences in the United States are large, at least compared to other differences thought to be important, see, for instance, Hero, *The Southerner and World Affairs*; Broom and Glenn, "Negro-White Differences in Reported Attitudes and Behavior"; Glenn, "Massification vs. Differentiation," and "Recent Trends in Inter-category Differences in Attitudes"; Glenn and Simmons, "Are Regional Cultural Differences Diminishing?"; and Reed, *The Enduring South*.

13. See Reed, *The Enduring South*, pp. 21–32. The adjectives were among those used in a classic study of ethnic stereotypes by Katz and Braley, "Racial Stereotypes of One Hundred College Students." Interviewers were supplied with synonyms where pretesting indicated that some of the words might not be understood by respondents. For each item, the stereotypic response was scored 2, responses of "no difference" and "don't know" were scored 1, and counter-

Figure 3.1 shows the relation between an index that measures the likelihood of thinking about regional differences in these conventional terms and exposure to the non-South. (Note that the "Extensive Exposure" category is defined somewhat differently from that in the index used in Table 3.4.) A majority (57 percent) of those who have lived outside the South for up to six years score high on the index, more than twice the proportion (27 percent) of those who have never been outside the South.[14] However, those with a great deal of experience outside the South are somewhat *less* likely to generalize in these terms than those with only an intermediate amount, a result giving additional support for the idea that although some people may know too little to stereotype, others seem to know too much.

This reversal at the upper end of the exposure continuum replicates the more usual finding about the effects of interaction across group boundaries on stereotyping: at the extreme end of the continuum, the so-called contact hypothesis works as specified and exposure reduces stereotyping. But before interaction can break down stereotypes, there must be stereotypes to break down. Our data suggest that many Southerners do not have stereotypes of Northerners before they actually encounter them, presumably because their regional status is simply not salient, because, that is, their regional consciousness is too low. This interpretation is supported by the results of a study by Gail Wood, who, with a sample of college students and rather different measures of both stereotyping and exposure, found exactly the same inverse-U-shaped relation as that reported here. The Southern students in her study reported that their principal source of information about Northerners was "personal contact," unlike the Northern students, who more often said they formed their impressions from books and

---

stereotypic responses were scored 0. A "high" score in Figure 3.1 is one of 16 or more, which means the respondent gave the stereotypic response to a majority of the items.

14. The effects of education are similar. We have seen that it increases regional consciousness, and it also increases the tendency to stereotype. Within each educational category, the curvilinear relation between exposure and stereotyping holds up. See Reed, *One South*, p. 130.

especially from movies. (For the Northern students, incidentally, the relation between exposure and stereotyping was straightforwardly negative, as might be expected if books and movies had already brought Southerners to their attention.)[15]

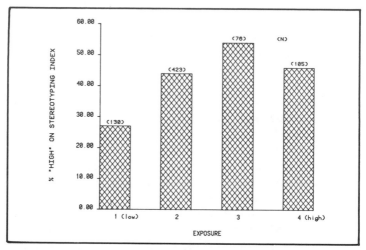

Figure 3.1. Relation of Stereotyping to Exposure

SOURCE: John Shelton Reed, "Getting to Know You: The Contact Hypothesis Applied to the Sectional Beliefs and Attitudes of White Southerners," *Social Forces* 59, no. 1 (September 1980): 129, fig. 1.

1. Never Been outside South: Southern-born, never lived outside South (eleven Confederate states, Kentucky, and Oklahoma), longest distance traveled from present home is less than 500 miles.

2. Traveled in North: Southern-born, never lived outside South, longest distance traveled is over 500 miles. (Note: For some respondents, this travel may have been entirely in the South. It is impossible to tell from the survey items available.)

3. Lived in North: Southern-born or border state-born, lived up to six years outside South (unless included in 4 below).

4. Extensive Exposure to North: Northern-born, or one or more years of schooling in North, or lived in North more than six years.

15. Wood, "The Images of Southern Males and Females."

Regional Consciousness and the "Traditional Value Orientation"

There is an interesting paradox here. If we ask what Southerners are most conscious of their Southernness, most likely to be aware of regional differences and prepared to generalize about them, most likely to have well-defined ideas about their regional group and their place in it, the answer appears to be that these properties are most common among "New Southerners"—educated, well-traveled, fairly "sophisticated," urban folks. Since more and more Southerners fit this description, it would seem that at least the short-run consequences of the South's economic development, urbanization, and general modernization will be to *raise* the level of regional consciousness and regional stereotyping among Southerners, not to lower it.

If there is a sense in which educated, mobile, urban Southerners are more "Southern" than before, however, there are also ways in which they are less so. Southerners, by and large, have been and still are set off from other Americans by a distinctive set of attitudes and values.[16] But some of these regional differences are decreasing and may indeed be disappearing. Many aspects of Southern culture have reflected a rural economy and society, poor education and little of it, and isolation from the outside world. In those respects, Southerners are becoming more "American" with each passing decade. Harold Grasmick, in a study of support for George Wallace based on the "Survey of North Carolina," identified a cluster of these variables and labeled them *the* "traditional value orientation," not just of the South but of folk and peasant societies in general (which is what the South has been, in the American context, until quite recently).[17] He developed measures of familism, localism, fatalism, resistance to innovation, tradi-

16. See n. 12 above.

17. Grasmick, "Social Change and the Wallace Movement in the South." As Howard Odum remarked: "The way of the South has been and is the way of the folk. The culture of the South is the culture of the folk" (*The Way of the South*, pp. 61–62). For a similar observation by an historian, see Potter, *The South and the Sectional Conflict*, p. 15.

tional sex-role ideology, racism, some aspects of authoritarianism, and suspicion and dislike of "outsiders" (in the Southern case, some aspects of sectionalism); and his review of the literature on modernization concluded that these traits have characterized preindustrial societies throughout the world. His data showed that they are widespread in the "preindustrial" parts of the South's population as well. In particular, he showed that the traditional value orientation is strongly related to three factors: growing up on a farm, the absence of education, and the absence of a cluster of variables he called "late socialization experiences"—urban residence, travel and residence outside the South, and exposure to the mass media. (He found that old people were more likely to hold traditional values than young people, and women more likely than men, but he was able to demonstrate that these differences were entirely due to differences in background and experience between old and young people and between men and women.)

He also found that all of the components of the traditional value orientation tended to vary together: for instance, someone who displayed a high level of fatalism was also likely to hold racist attitudes, and vice versa. All of the traits that make up the traditional value orientation were concentrated in the same elements of the population and appeared to have the same correlates: immersion in the traditional rural culture of the South and isolation from the influences of education, city life, travel, and the mass media.

Using the items that Grasmick identified as indicators of this value orientation (excluding those that asked about the South per se) and using the weights he devised, I constructed an index similar to his. (Appendix B describes this index in more detail.) The index was dichotomized: the top 58 percent of white Southern respondents were considered to show high traditionalism. Table 3.5 shows some of the relevant results. Although these values have not been the only ones that, on the average, have distinguished Southerners from other Americans, they certainly have made up a large part of the historic stereotype of Southerners and a conspicuous and often politically significant component of the

Table 3.5. Relation of Traditional Value Orientation Index to Background and Experience Variables

Variable	High Traditionalism	(N)
Male	53%	(336)
Female	56%	(404)
Middle class (self-reported)	47%	(251)
Working class (self-reported)	72%	(329)
"Don't think in terms of classes"	46%	(160)
Income under $5,000	81%	(194)
Income between $5,000 and $10,000	58%	(255)
Income over $10,000	36%	(248)
Less than high school education	78%	(340)
High school graduate	45%	(315)
College graduate	22%	(85)
Urban or suburban residence	54%	(455)
Rural residence	64%	(285)
Professional or managerial workers	27%	(59)
Clerical or sales workers	41%	(182)
Skilled laborers and operatives	45%	(62)
Unskilled and service workers	68%	(145)
Farmers and farm laborers	71%	(14)
Watched television news day before	51%	(367)
Did not watch television news day before	64%	(371)
Read newspaper in last two days	52%	(563)
Did not read newspaper in last two days	75%	(176)
Went to library in past year	39%	(231)
Did not go to library in past year	66%	(508)
Born in South	60%	(704)
Born in border states	44%	(9)
Born outside South	11%	(27)
No schooling outside South	61%	(667)
One year or less non-Southern schooling	53%	(30)
1–5 years non-Southern schooling	32%	(19)
6+ years non-Southern schooling	8%	(24)
No travel more than 200 miles away	91%	(23)
Travel 200–500 miles from home	74%	(115)
Travel 500 miles from home	51%	(595)
No residence outside South	59%	(639)
Residence outside South	39%	(101)
Low exposure	82%	(141)
Traveled in North	56%	(462)
Lived in North	51%	(59)
High exposure	32%	(78)

actual regional difference. In this sample, the index clearly distin-
guishes the Northern-born respondents. Despite the fact that the
base is restricted to those who say that they think of themselves as
Southerners, only 11 percent of them score high on the index,
compared to three out of five of the Southern-born. Presumably
other Northern-born residents of the South (and non-Southerners
in general) also display low levels of these traditional values.

Table 3.5 also shows (as Grasmick reported) that traditionalism
is inversely related to education, income, urban residence, media
exposure, experience outside the South, and so forth. In other
words, *the very same factors that increase regional consciousness
decrease the likelihood that one will subscribe to "Southern" values*—if we take those values to be racism, localism, authoritarianism, and the other components of Grasmick's traditional value
orientation.

The fact that the same social forces that heighten Southerners'
regional consciousness also chip away at the traditional value orientation may help to account for the otherwise puzzling fact that
regional consciousness is essentially uncorrelated with those traditional values, as Table 3.6 shows.[18] That is, those who are most
traditional are no more likely than others to display high regional
consciousness, or, put the other way around, those Southerners
who are most self-conscious have no more to be self-conscious
about than other Southerners.

Since regional consciousness and traditionalism are strongly related, in opposite directions, to the same set of experiences and
background variables, the absence of an association between the
two does not mean that they have nothing to do with one another.
On the contrary, when we look at Southerners who are similar in
terms of upbringing, education, travel, media exposure, and the
like, higher levels of traditionalism should be reflected in higher

18. Compare these results to those from the analysis of a 1963 Southwide survey, which found only a slight positive association, and that almost entirely spu-
rious, between a measure of something resembling what we are calling regional
consciousness and support for racial segregation (an important component of
Grasmick's traditional value orientation); see Reed, *One South*, chap. 5, "The
Cardinal Test of a Southerner?"

Table 3.6. Regional Consciousness by Traditionalism

Regional Consciousness	Traditionalism	
	Low	High
High (3–4)	38%	39%
Medium (2)	25	25
Low (0–1)	37	37
Total	100%	101%*
(N)	(317)	(412)

*Total differs from 100% due to rounding error.

levels of regional consciousness. The causal link between these two variables is masked by their quite different relations to the antecedent variables. Table 3.7 shows what happens when education and exposure are controlled. Although the percentage bases are too small to inspire confidence in most cases, in seven of the eight comparisons of groups similar in these respects and large enough to compare percentages, consciousness increases as traditionalism does. Additional controls for the other background variables should produce an even stronger positive association.

Four Types of Southerners

But the fact that traditionalism and regional consciousness are causally related does not change the fact that they are not statistically associated in the population from which our sample comes. The typology in Figure 3.2 is of course an oversimplification, since both regional consciousness and the value dimension are continua rather than dichotomies, but it may help to clarify some implications of the fact that the two variables are uncorrelated. (The labels for the quadrants are perhaps too precious as well, but they will serve to identify the types.) Since the two variables that define the typology are virtually uncorrelated, if we define "high" and "low" in the figure to mean "above the median" and "below

Table 3.7. Regional Consciousness by Traditionalism, Controlling for Education and Exposure

		Percentage with High Consciousness (3–4) (N)	
Education	Exposure	Low Traditionalism	High Traditionalism
Not high school graduate	Low	27% (11)	17% (81)
	Traveled in North	31% (52)	40% (159)
	Lived in North	44% (9)	46% (24)
High school graduate	Low	31% (13)	38% (32)
	Traveled in North	40% (111)	41% (86)
	Lived in North	44% (45)	67% (24)
College graduate	Low	* (1)	* (2)
	Traveled in North	39% (38)	60% (10)
	Lived in North	46% (24)	86% (7)

*Base too small for computation of reliable percentage.

the median" respectively, then all four types exist in roughly equal numbers in the population.

We can speculate about the nature of the long-term shifts from one quadrant to another. A plausible sequence, on the face of it, would be for economic and demographic change in the South—more education, cities, money, travel, mass media, and so forth—to move the bulk of the Southern population inexorably from the

Figure 3.2. Southern Types, Defined by Level of Regional Consciousness and Adherence to Traditional Value Orientation

Traditional Value Orientation	Regional Consciousness	
	High	Low
High	"Fire-eater"	"Local" ("Peasant")
Low	"New Southerner"	"Cosmopolitan"

upper-left quadrant to the lower-right, from "fire-eaters" who espouse traditional values and think of themselves parochially as Southerners to "cosmopolitan" moderns who are not distinctively Southern in any of the important respects Grasmick identified and for whom the South is nothing but a place to live.

The data, however, do not allow this simple evolutionary picture. For many, the starting place is not the "fire-eater" quadrant but the "local" one: although these people possess the "peasant" characteristics that Grasmick enumerated, they also share with peasants elsewhere in the world the characteristic of narrow horizons, horizons too narrow for them to give much attention to a concept as abstract as "the South" or to think of themselves often as part of it. Those who lack regional consciousness may not be cosmopolitans at all, far from it. The starting point for many Southerners, it appears, is "localism"—in Robert Merton's definition, "an orientation to local social structures." [19] This orientation produces adherence to local values, the traditional value orientation of the South, but at the same time it works against a more cosmopolitan recognition that these are *Southern* values, that is, against regional consciousness.

What forces are at work to move people out of the "local" quadrant in our typology? Historically, we can identify two dis-

19. The analysis of the 1963 study mentioned above found that those Southerners who scored low on the measure of regional consciousness were no more likely

tinct processes, one intermittent and operating in the short run, and the other long-term and more lasting in its effects, but neither leading directly to cosmopolitanism. In the first place, the sectional conflict that has been a frequent characteristic of American life—most notably, of course, during the Civil War and its aftermath, but off and on before and since—must operate to heighten regional consciousness.[20] When the South as a whole is seen to be a contestant on the national stage, when Southerners collectively have (or are seen to have) common interests in need of expression or defense, the salience of the regional group—that is, regional consciousness—will be increased for its members. But short-term sectional conflict increases consciousness without presenting any fundamental threat to the traditional value orientation; indeed, it may reinforce it, particularly those aspects of it that serve as "badges" of sectional identity setting Southerners off from their adversaries and those that reflect ethnocentrism, fear and suspicion of "outsiders." Sectional conflict, it would seem, moves people from the right-hand quadrants in Figure 3.2 to the left-hand ones, turning "locals" into "fire-eaters" and perhaps even turning "cosmopolitans" into "New Southerners," if not "fire-eaters" themselves.

But the effects of sectional conflict are presumably temporary. We may suppose that there is a sociological equivalent of the Second Law of Thermodynamics that leads groups (including re-

---

than those with higher levels of consciousness to follow national and international news in the mass media, but much more likely to attend to strictly *local* news; see Reed, *One South*, chap. 5, "The Cardinal Test of a Southerner?" Robert Merton introduced the terms "local" and "cosmopolitan" to the sociological lexicon in his *Social Theory and Social Structure*, pp. 392–420. See also Gouldner, "Cosmopolitans and Locals."

20. That conflict strengthens group boundaries and raises the consciousness of group members is almost a sociological commonplace. The relation between social conflict and individual consciousness has been discussed by Georg Simmel and Robert Park, among others. See Coser, *The Functions of Social Conflict*. Blumer's discussion of the "big event" and its effects on group identity is especially pertinent here; see "Race Prejudice as a Sense of Group Position," p. 6. Shibutani has also dealt with this subject in "On the Personification of Adversaries," elaborating on Erich Voegelin's concept of *die Gegenidee*.

gional groups) to dissolve in the absence of at least intermittent reinforcement. When sectional conflict abates (as it always has, eventually), individuals forget; if individuals do not forget, new generations come along who never knew. Without the recurrent stimulus of regional conflict, one important element in the matrix of regional consciousness will be lacking. Opinions differ about whether we are likely to see the end of sectional conflict any time soon.

Our earlier analysis suggests, however, that there is another process by which the regional consciousness of Southerners is heightened, both for many individuals within their lifetimes and for succeeding generations. It depends less on the relations between sections at the national level than on the experiences and circumstances of individual Southerners. Urbanization, education, the prevalence of the mass media, and social and geographical mobility—all increasingly widespread among Southerners—can heighten regional consciousness at the same time that they undermine the traditional value orientation. More and more, these experiences are moving Southerners from the "local" quadrant of the table and making "New Southerners" of them; one must also assume that Southern children are increasingly *born* in that quadrant.

The changes produced by modernization will probably prove to be irreversible. To revert to a lost traditional value orientation is difficult, if not impossible, as nationalist regimes from Ireland to Iran have discovered. It remains to be seen whether the awkward age represented by the "New Southerner" quadrant—heightened consciousness with diminished differences—is a terminus or merely a way station on the route to cosmopolitanism. However, it does appear to be at least a necessary intermediate step. It is this condition—not deracination but a sort of marginality—that is the characteristic modern predicament, and not just in the "New South."

CHAPTER 4

"My Kind of People"

Regional Identification

We saw in chapter 2 that some of those who rejected Southern affiliation—who said, despite their residential histories, that they were not Southerners—did so on the grounds that they had little in common with "real" Southerners or even disliked them. This is one extreme of a continuum that one can call regional *identification*, a variable related both conceptually and empirically to a sense of empathy with other group members and closeness to them. We may suppose that this variable will be related both to regional consciousness (some degree of which must be at least a prerequisite for identification) and to one's actual, objective similarity to other Southerners, although someone can "look" very Southern culturally without realizing it.

The survey did not contain a great many items suitable for measuring identification, but three seem to capture most of what I wish the term "identification" to convey. Some examination of the responses to these questions and the reasons people gave for responding as they did may help to justify the choice of items.

The first was worded as follows: "Some people in the South feel they have a lot in common with other Southerners; but others we talk to don't feel that way so much. How about you? Would you say you feel pretty close to Southerners in general or that you

don't feel much closer to them than to other people?"[1] Fifty-seven
percent of our respondents said they felt "pretty close" to Southerners; among those who thought of themselves as Southerners,
the figure was 65 percent.

The other two items in the index are measures of "in-group
preference," a stated preference for other Southerners in hypothetical forced-choice situations. Respondents were asked:

> Suppose you are the manager of a company which must
> hire a scientist. Two persons apply: one born and educated
> in the North, the other born and educated in the South. If
> they were equally qualified, which would you prefer: the
> Northerner or the Southerner?

> Suppose that two good men are running for Congressman
> in your district, but one of them was born and raised in the
> South, the other born and raised in the North. If each man
> had moved to the district five years ago, which one would
> you favor?

We tried to equate the candidates in all respects except region of
origin (both Congressional candidates were "outsiders," for instance, but one was a Southern and one a Northern outsider), but
there is some evidence that these rather subtle manipulations were
lost on some of our respondents. Nevertheless, as we shall see, a
strong affective element colored the responses to these questions,

---

1. Technically, this is called a "double-barreled" question since it confounds
having "a lot in common" with other Southerners with feeling "closer to them
than to other people," but that confusion may be almost desirable in this case since
both are aspects of identification. This question was one of two used by Campbell
and his colleagues in *The American Voter* to measure "group identification." I
have used the second item, "How much interest would you say you have in how
[other group members] are getting along in this country?" to validate our measure
of consciousness, since it seems to have more to do with that than with identification, in the more restrictive sense in which I am using that word. With *The American Voter*'s index of group identification, white Southerners can be shown to have
a high average level of that variable, compared to the levels for other groups this
question has been addressed to: higher than that for Roman Catholics and union
members, approaching the levels displayed by Jews and by black Americans. See
Reed, *The Enduring South*, pp. 10–11.

and they seem to have picked up an additional aspect of what I mean by regional identification.

Note that these questions *forced a choice*. They measured less hostility and prejudice against Northerners than preference for Southerners, when other things were equal and when a choice had to be made. In chapter 6 we shall turn to the obviously related question of anti-Northern prejudice. As Table 4.1 shows, respondents were about evenly divided between those who would prefer the Southerner in each situation and those who volunteered that they would not care or that their choice would depend on some other factor. Small minorities said that they would choose the Northerner or that they could not answer the question. Not surprisingly, those respondents who had said earlier that they were not Southerners were less likely to choose the Southerner (strikingly so, when faced with hiring a scientist) and roughly five times as likely as Southerners to choose the Northerner.

Responses to the follow-up question, "Why did you choose the Southerner [or Northerner]?" indicated clearly that these questions tapped an aspect of regional identification. Nearly half of those who chose the Southerner for the technical position indi-

Table 4.1. Distributions of Preferences, for Total Sample and for Self-Designated Southerners and Non-Southerners

	Preference				
	South-erner	Don't care, depends	North-erner	Don't know, can't say	(N)
For Job as Scientist					
Total Sample	41%	46	6	6	(891)
Southerners	46%	44	4	6	(732)
Non-Southerners	15%	60	20	5	(116)
For Congressman					
Total Sample	42%	47	3	8	(890)
Southerners	45%	47	2	7	(731)
Non-Southerners	30%	49	11	10	(116)

cated that they did so out of a sense of community with him. These responses were typical:

"Because *I'm* a Southerner."

"Just because he was a Southerner and I am a Southerner."

"He's a Southerner—I'm a Southerner. I thought I'd give him a break."

"Because of loyalty to the South. I don't have any grudge against the Northerner, though. I would just give the Southerner a break."

"The South's awakening and needs a little boost. It would be easier for the Northerner to find a place somewhere else."

"[I would like to] keep our good people in the South instead of their going north for jobs."

"Because he is 'home folks.'"

"I would feel empathy with him."

"I feel a relationship to a Southerner."

"We would have more in common. Temperament and disposition would be more the same."

"I would say for me he would be easier to communicate with."

"We could understand each other better."

Like the last of these responses, which may refer to the candidate's accent rather than his way of thinking, many of these answers shade into another category of reasons for choosing the Southern scientist. About a third of those who did so gave answers that implied that the Southerner *would do a better job*, not because of superior technical qualifications but because of imputed personality traits and social skills. These respondents would hire the Southerner because they felt that he would get along better with Southern employees, understand the "Southern way" of doing things, or share stereotypical "Southern traits" that would make him a better employee. Some of these responses may not indicate regional identification at all: if the perceptions on which they are based are accurate, the preference may be as strictly instrumental as that of one respondent who said that the Southerner would work for lower pay. Still, most of these responses have a distinct affective flavor. These examples will give some idea of the range of responses:

"Southerners are better rounded and get along better with people."

"Because Yankees are too damn hard to get along with."

"As a rule, [Southerners] use more common sense in dealing with other people."

"He would get along better with the [other] people. They would understand him better."

"He would fit better—more congenial and compatible."

"Because [Southerners] are more congenial generally. . . . I guess I am more attached to the South than I thought I was."

"Social life would be easier and more compatible [with a Southerner]."

"Because Southerners are more solid—they can be reasoned with. A Northerner comes down here and everything must be his way."

"A Southerner seems to me like an all-round better person. A Southerner usually has a lot of common sense. A Northerner is selfish, out to get what he can for himself."

"Yankees ought to stay where they belong. They don't seem to have any common sense."

"I had a boss who was from the North and he felt that he knew it all."

"Northerners are too bossy and pushy."

"Northerners sound too bossy. They're short-talking people and sound bossy when they don't really mean to be, I believe."

"[Southerners] are more courteous. Really, I just don't much like Northerners, their language. I don't like to work around them."

"Because [the Southerner] is more concerned with people."

"I believe there would be a sense of loyalty and gentleman-liness about a Southern man, which is a general Southern trait."

"Southern people are a little more stable. Northern people are too fast, too fly-by-night."

"Because I believe he will work at a more natural pace and be more productive than an aggressive person."

"I think [Southerners] are more down-to-earth."

"Southerners are better able to cope with the Southern way of life."

"Because [the Southerner] would understand Southern problems."

"I just think he would know more about this part of the country. He'd know how to act."

Notice how many of these responses imply that Southerners *understand* one another better than they understand Northerners or Northerners them. For every respondent who seems to dislike Northerners, there are many more who simply find them difficult to understand or believe that Northerners do not understand Southerners. This greater ease of communication, sharing of a code, is certainly one element of what we mean by group identification. Indeed, Karl Deutsch has argued that a community of communication should be used to define a *nation*, although presumably the barriers to communication outside the group must be greater than those between Southerners and other Americans.[2]

As Table 4.1 shows, most of those who did not choose the Southerner indicated that it did not matter, a response that it seems reasonable to suppose indicates the absence of strong regional identification. Among the small minority who chose the Northerner, a few (mostly migrants) indicated identification with *him*:

> "I don't know—I'm just attracted to people from the North."

> "I put more faith in people from the North."

> "I think he'd be easier [for me] to get along with."

> "'Cause I wished *I* was a Northerner."

Most of those who chose the Northern applicant, however, did so because they assumed he would have stereotypical qualities that would make him better suited for the job (despite the "equally qualified" proviso in the question):

> "The best scientific training is in the North."

> "They're better educated and have a better outlook on things and are smarter."

> "He'd know more about science and industry [and] have more experience."

> "They are more up-to-date on things than Southerners."

> "I feel he'd probably have the better education."

> "They go in for scientific knowledge more."

> "I feel like even if both are equally qualified, the North is a bit ahead of the South in education and research."

Besides "going in for scientific knowledge more," Northerners were seen as more ambitious and harder workers:

2. Deutsch, *Nationalism and Social Communication*.

"Northerners seem to be more aggressive."

"The Northerner can do it better and faster."

"[He] would apply himself more, [have] a better attitude."

"Because I've found down here the people aren't so ambitious and don't strive for education as the Northerners do."

"He would get the job done while the Southerner is thinking about it."

"Because he is more interested in getting ahead and doing a better job."

"Guess I feel like I'd get more work out of him, being from the North."

A quarter of those who chose the Northerner mentioned their man's superior technical qualifications or willingness to work, compared to only 2 percent of those who chose the Southerner. As we saw in chapter 3, not all aspects of the Southern stereotype of Northerners are unflattering, and any sense of regional identification these respondents might feel is outweighed by instrumental considerations based on that stereotype.

Since the technical qualifications for being a congressman were less widely agreed upon than those for being a scientist, such reasons were less often given as the basis for choosing one of the hypothetical candidates for Congress. The few who chose the Northern-raised man did so for a variety of reasons: a few mentioned again that Northerners are smarter or at least better educated; one felt that the Northerner would probably be more sympathetic to organized labor; a few felt that he would be more aggressive or "pushy" and that this was a desirable quality in a congressman. But most of those who chose the Northerner did so simply because they liked Northerners or disliked Southerners.

Those who chose the Southern candidate gave much the same reasons for their choices as those who chose the Southern scientist: a feeling of empathy with other Southerners or a sense that the Southerner would be more approachable or congenial than the Northerner. Some felt that the Southerner's upbringing would help him understand and represent "Southern interests" in Congress, interests that presumably transcended those of their particular congressional district. As one (white) respondent put it: "We niggers down here have to stick together."

Whether it is based on shared interests or shared culture, however, the sense of identification this question taps is similar to that elicited by the other two questions in our index. The two forced-choice items show a respectable correlation with one another (tau-b = .34), and each has a modest correlation with the item asking about closeness to other Southerners (tau-b = .19 for the scientist item, .15 for the congressman). We used responses to these three questions to construct a simple additive index, with the closeness question scored zero or two, for no or yes, and the choice questions scored zero if the Northerner was chosen, one if the respondent said it made no difference, and two if the Southerner was chosen. Twenty-one percent of our respondents displayed the highest level of identification: they chose the Southern candidate in both situations and indicated that they felt closer to Southerners than to other people. Another 20 percent had the next highest score on the index: in one of the choice situations, they said that region made no difference.

Identification and Consciousness

Although what we are calling "identification" is conceptually distinct from "consciousness"—the first having to do with feeling, the second with cognition—there is good reason to expect the two phenomena to be empirically related. It would seem almost prerequisite that some degree of thought about the South and one's place in it should attend the sense that one has something in common with other Southerners and a consequent feeling of closeness to them. In addition, given that a group exists in someone's mind, a feeling of identification with it should ordinarily increase its salience.

In fact, our measures of the two concepts are positively related, but the relation is far from perfect, as we see when the two indexes are cross-tabulated in Table 4.2. There are representatives of both deviant types: not only Southerners who give some thought to the matter but do not feel particularly close to other Southerners, but those who acknowledge (when asked) identification with the group, although they have not thought much about it.

Identification is not strongly related to the sorts of backgrounds and experiences that we found to be related to consciousness (positively) and to traditionalism (negatively). Table 4.3 shows some of the relevant associations. Identification shows a noticeable association only with education: it increases somewhat as education increases. It is hardly related at all to experience outside the South or to media exposure.

The reason for this, and for the relatively weak association between identification and consciousness, is that identification is also related to the traditional value orientation. Figure 4.1 shows the somewhat complicated causal connections that appear to be operating. The modernizing, consciousness-raising backgrounds and experiences that we examined in chapter 3 operate both to increase identification, by increasing consciousness, and to decrease it, by decreasing the traditional value orientation, thus making people "look" less Southern, culturally, and causing them to have less "in common with other Southerners" objectively.

Table 4.2. Identification, by Consciousness

	Consciousness				
	Low				High
Identification	0	1	2	3	4
High 6	12%	12%	18%	23%	41%
5	6	22	24	20	26
4	29	30	33	37	23
3	18	15	8	9	5
Low 0–2	35	22	17	11	5
Total	100%	101%*	100%	100%	100%
(N)	(78)	(186)	(179)	(147)	(128)

*Total differs from 100% due to rounding error.

Table 4.3. Identification, by Selected Variables Tapping Exposure to Non-Southern Culture

	High Identification	(N)
Born outside South	46%	(24)
Born in South	42%	(696)
School attendance outside South	41%	(69)
No school attendance outside South	42%	(648)
Not a high school graduate	39%	(337)
High school graduate	43%	(311)
College graduate	49%	(81)
Watched television news today or yesterday	44%	(362)
Did not watch television news today or yesterday	40%	(365)
Read newspaper today or yesterday	42%	(554)
Did not read newspaper today or yesterday	43%	(174)
Went to library in past year	41%	(225)
Did not go to library in past year	42%	(503)

Table 4.4 shows the effects of different combinations of consciousness and traditionalism on identification. Among those Southerners with high regional consciousness, the absence of traditional values greatly reduces identification. Among those with lower levels of regional consciousness, the absence of traditional values makes less difference. Put another way, although both consciousness and traditionalism contribute to regional identification, when both are present, identification is especially likely. In terms of the simplistic typology from chapter 3, the highest levels of regional identification are displayed by the "fire-eaters," those who accept the traditional value orientation and have high levels

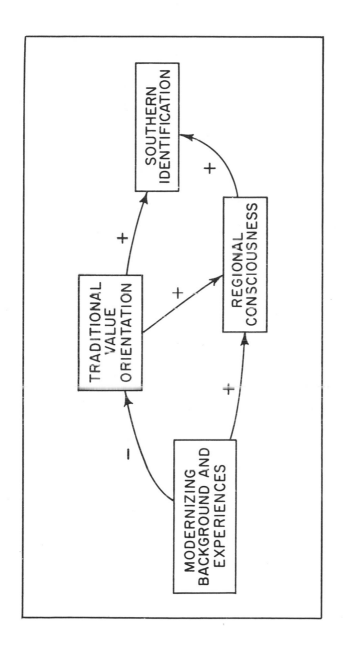

Figure 4.1. Antecedents of Regional Identification

of regional consciousness. Of the sixty-seven respondents who scored the highest on the consciousness index and also scored high on the traditionalism index, 74 percent scored high (five or six) on the identification index and a majority (51 percent) had the highest possible score. Among "New Southerners," those with similarly high consciousness levels who scored low on traditionalism, only 59 percent showed high identification and only 31 percent had the highest possible identification score. They are evidently less convinced than the "fire-eaters" that they have the things in common with other Southerners necessary for *really* high levels of identification. "Cosmopolitans," those with low regional consciousness and low levels of the traditional value orientation, have the lowest levels of regional identification, and the "locals," who share the traditional value orientation but lack regional consciousness, have levels of identification almost as low.

Table 4.4. Identification, by Consciousness and Traditionalism

		Percentage with High Identification (5–6) (N)	
Consciousness		High Traditionalism	Low Traditionalism
		"Locals"	*"Cosmopolitans"*
Low	0	19%	16%
		(53)	(25)
	1	33%	33%
		(102)	(84)
	2	39%	46%
		(103)	(76)
	3	44%	42%
		(94)	(53)
High	4	74%	59%
		(67)	(61)
		"Fire-eaters"	*"New Southerners"*

So what are the implications for regional identification in the South? If the only genuinely endangered species in this typology is the "local," the short-run forecast is for average levels of regional identification at least as high as we have seen in the past. The immediate destination for locals driven from that quadrant by the forces of modernization is not "cosmopolitanism," the only type for which regional identification is lower. At the same time, however, to the extent that regional identification hinges on the traditional value orientation as an ethnic marker, to the extent that those values are what Southerners think about when asked if they have things in common with other Southerners, the long-term prognosis is not favorable. But who is to say that the traditional value orientation is the only marker that can serve? Perhaps regional identification is based even now on factors other than a shared culture: common interests, common grievances, a common inheritance of a real or imagined history. We shall consider that possibility in the next chapter.

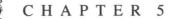

CHAPTER 5

"Not Forgotten"

Southern Grievances, Southern History, and Symbolic Sectionalism

Southernness, like the identity of many other groups but perhaps more so, has been shaped and reinforced by conflict. For Southerners, this conflict has been with "the North," that is, the rest of the United States. Southern identity (and, some have suggested, much of Southern culture) was and probably remains a reactive adaptation to a state of intermittent sectional conflict.[1] Since the South has usually lost these battles and since Southerners have liked to believe they did not start them (their historic wish being simply to be "left alone"), it is not surprising that some have detected a sense of grievance at the heart of Southern identity, a sense of ill-treatment at the hands of the rest of the country.

The clearest statement of this proposition comes from Sheldon Hackney (who combines the perspectives of an Alabamian, a professional historian, and an Ivy League university president). Being Southern, he has written, "inevitably involves a feeling of persecution at times and a sense of being a passive, insignificant object of alien or impersonal forces." The origins of Southern self-consciousness lie in the antebellum "need to protect a pecu-

1. For a summary, see Reed, *The Enduring South*, pp. 88–90.

liar institution from threats originating outside the region," so "Southern identity has been linked from the first to a siege mentality." Southerners, of course, have other identities than their regional one, but "they are likely to be most conscious of being Southerners when they are defending their region against attack from outside forces: abolitionists, the Union Army, carpetbaggers, Wall Street and Pittsburgh, civil rights agitators, the federal government, feminism, socialism, trade-unionism, Darwinism, Communism, atheism, daylight-saving time, and other by-products of modernity." Hackney was not being entirely facetious: most of these adversaries are real enough. As he acknowledged, "almost every significant change in the life of the South has been initiated by external powers." Small wonder, perhaps, that some Southerners display "an extreme sensitivity to criticism from outsiders and a tendency to excuse local faults as the products of forces beyond human or local control." [2]

I do not wish to dwell here on the question of whether the South has been mistreated, but cannot resist one story. On the "Tonight Show" a few years back, Jerry Lewis remarked that while flying to New York he had used the rest room over Mississippi, "fulfilling a long-standing ambition." His remark may suggest that Southerners, at least Mississippians, do not share the immunities that the media confer on most racial, religious, and nationality groups. The response (the governor called for, and got, an apology, a congressman demanded an investigation, and a Mississippi NBC affiliate canceled the Jerry Lewis program) suggests that Southerners share the sensitivity to slights, perhaps exaggerated and self-defeating, of these other groups. [3]

2. Hackney, "Southern Violence," pp. 924–25. Others have suggested different outcomes from this same history of frustration and defeat, notably C. Vann Woodward, in *The Burden of Southern History*. Woodward's argument that Southerners' history has given them a sense of tragedy and of irony—that is, that Southerners have learned from history—is fundamentally more optimistic than Hackney's view. Killian presents a discussion of "defensive group identity" among Southerners that is very similar to Hackney's position (*White Southerners*, especially pp. 142–44).

3. Glen Elder called this story to my attention. It can be found in an Associated

Whether a sense of grievance is justified or not, many Southerners feel it. If group consciousness and identification are heightened by conflict, it may well be that the highest level can be found among those who believe that the conflict is an ongoing one, although whether the belief precedes or follows identification is not clear. These data allow us to explore the subject a bit.

Southern Complaints

Historically, Southern grievance against the North has been aired in three related areas: economic, political, and (for lack of a better word) cultural.[4] Lewis's affront was "cultural," revealing a lack of respect. Our data suggest that at present the most salient grievance is the cultural one: many Southerners mightily resent what they see (to a large extent correctly) as the Northern stereotype of Southerners. One Tennesseean wrote about this problem to columnist Ann Landers: "I am getting fed up with hearing all Southerners lumped together and described as bigots, rednecks, racists, etc. . . . We Southerners are not the ignoramuses portrayed on television. People who have preconceived notions about us are the REAL ignoramuses. They ought to come down here and look us over. They'd learn something."[5] This sense of being regarded as inferior comes across quite clearly in the survey responses. Although only about a quarter of our respondents agreed that "most Northerners dislike Southerners" and half disagreed (the others

---

Press release of 27 April 1969. Many Southerners also dump on Mississippi, of course, but seldom so literally and usually entre nous.

4. Seldom have these complaints been voiced so articulately as by the Vanderbilt Agrarians, in *I'll Take My Stand*, by Twelve Southerners, and in their subsequent writings. For a summary and discussion, see Reed, "For Dixieland: The Sectionalism of *I'll Take My Stand*." These three areas of grievance correspond roughly to Max Weber's dimensions of social stratification; see Weber's "Class, Status, and Party."

5. *Greensboro Daily News*, 26 November 1972, p. D-12. Miss Landers replied, "Dear Tenn.: You speak the truth." Roy Blount, Jr., offers some further observations on "the ignoramuses portrayed on television" in "C'mon, They're Not All Dumber Than Two-Dollar Dogs!"

were uncertain), about half agreed that "most Northerners *look down on* Southerners" and only one in three disagreed.

We failed to include any open-ended questions to let our respondents express their resentment, but some voiced it anyway, and our interviewers had the presence of mind to record some of their observations. A twenty-three-year-old bookkeeper and secretary remarked that "the South has *always* been looked down on." A middle-aged machine operator, the wife of a retired truck driver, volunteered that "they [Northerners] look down on Southerners as being dumb, but we're not." An eighty-four-year-old widow, a retired schoolteacher, agreed: "They pick on the South, and the papers, particularly, tell how awful we are here, but we're not." The belief that the South does not get an even break from the mass media is widespread. Although only a quarter of our respondents agreed that "national news programs on radio and television are nearly always unfair to the South" ("nearly always" may have been too strong, and the worst offenders may be dramas and situation comedies rather than news programs), close to half agreed that "books and magazine articles about the South play up its bad points and don't give a fair picture" and only a third disagreed. There is a clue here to one of the ways that exposure to the media can operate to increase regional consciousness. Many of our respondents feel that Southerners get no respect in the national conversation.

Another kind of deprivation that has been a historic focus for Southern discontent stems from the South's economic situation. In the Populist era and again in the 1920s and 1930s, many vocal Southerners attributed the South's economic underdevelopment to its quasi-colonial position in the United States and some (with more or less gusto) to exploitation by Northern capitalists.[6] There is some question, however, of the extent to which this analysis was shared by Southerners other than politicians and academics. Certainly our evidence indicates that it has little currency today.

6. See Tindall, *The Ethnic Southerners*, chap. 10, "The Colonial Economy and the Growth Psychology." This was one of the few things on which the Vanderbilt Agrarians and the Chapel Hill "regionalists" could agree (Vance, *Human Geography of the South*, pp. 467–76).

The majority of our respondents, in fact, see nothing to be explained. Even though they were interviewed before the idea of the "Sunbelt" was born, most did not believe that the South's economy was lagging. When asked "Who's doing better economically nowadays, Northerners or Southerners?" 54 percent said they saw no difference and another 14 percent said they did not know. (We also asked people to consider the statement: "The South is or soon will be as progressive as the rest of the country." Only 9 percent disagreed, a statistic relevant here if "progressive" is taken to include material well-being.) About a quarter of our respondents (28 percent) did allow that Northerners were currently better off economically than Southerners (only 4 percent thought Southerners were better off), but when asked why, most of them did not really address the question and gave responses such as "they have more money" or "got more work to do." Some restated the premise at the institutional level ("greater industrial capacity") without elaboration. When specific reasons were given, most (except for a handful who mentioned labor unionization) focused on Northerners' allegedly superior education ("I think their schools are better"; "The North is better educated"; "They're smarter") or on supposed cultural differences ("Southerners aren't as progressive and they're too prejudiced"; "Northerners are more aggressive—in fact, they're cutthroat").

Not one respondent gave an answer that could reasonably be construed as blaming the South's economic plight on a peripheral position in the world capitalist system or even on the machinations of Yankee capitalists. However, when we asked directly whether "Northern industry has been making a big profit off the South's natural resources, like coal and timber, with very little return to the South," 41 percent agreed and only 26 percent disagreed, an indication that the "colonial economy" argument still has some appeal, even if it is not one that Southerners make spontaneously. Although the South's economic situation does not weigh very heavily on people's minds these days, spontaneous, volunteered complaint is somewhat more in evidence when we turn to questions about the South's *political* situation. Although the survey antedated the election of Jimmy Carter and although we cannot say how that election and the subsequent history of the Carter administration affected these perceptions, a large minority of our respondents clearly felt that "Northerners have more power in Washington than is fair." More than a third (36 percent) said so, 41 percent thought they had about the right amount, and only 1 percent thought Northerners should have more power. Again, those who thought the South was deprived did not seem to have very clear ideas about *why*. When we asked why the North had more power than it should, a great many said it was because the North's population was larger, implying that Calhoun's doctrine of the concurrent majority may still have some appeal. A substantial minority, however, ascribed the South's lack of power to conscious discrimination against Southerners. I shall quote at length, to give a sense of the tone of these responses:

A sixty-year-old warehouse supervisor: "[Northerners] get together and seem to work against the South for some reason."

A thirty-three-year-old housewife: "Southerners have been walked on and no one up there [in Washington] listens to them."

A retired policeman: "Northern states won't go with the South."

A sixty-seven-year-old widowed housewife: "They try to keep all Southerners out of office."

A Baptist minister's wife, twenty-seven years old: "Seems like the Congress is always picking on the South and they let the North have their way."

A seventy-three-year-old real estate salesman: "Some of them seem to be still fighting the Civil War, still want to show us they're the boss."

The wife of an army sergeant, forty-three years old: "Seems like they pick on the South."

A construction company owner and machine operator, forty-nine years old: "Seems like all the political situations that come up, they seem to try to ram their opinions down the Southerners' throats."

The middle-aged wife of an insurance agent: "I don't think they pay much attention to Southerners. I think they're prejudiced against us."

A forty-five-year-old secretary and head of household: "I feel Northerners are prejudiced more against Southerners than Southerners against Northerners. Being a Southerner [works] against a man who is running for national office."

A middle-aged machine operator, wife of a retired truck driver: "The North doesn't want the South to have more power. They fight to keep the South out of power as much as possible."

A thirty-eight-year-old secretary, widowed mother of two children: "The Supreme Court is one of the best examples. They systematically excluded from the Court any Southerner who was nominated."

The last quotation refers to President Nixon's nominations of two Southern judges for a seat on the Supreme Court. Both were turned down by Congress, a rejection interpreted by much of the Southern press, and by President Nixon, as an expression of anti-Southern prejudice. As one middle-of-the-road North Carolina paper viewed it: "Liberal prejudice and anti-Southern bias have combined again to defeat confirmation to the Supreme Court of a Southern conservative. . . ." Six months later, the same paper was still licking its wounds: "Widespread prejudice against the South and Southerners not only denies them opportunities for service of which they are capable but denies to the nation their services which would be eminently useful and valuable to it." [7]

When we asked our respondents about their opinions of the matter after slightly over a year had passed, those who had an opinion were almost evenly divided over whether the two candi-

---

7. *Durham Morning Herald* editorials of 10 April and 31 October 1970.

dates were rejected because they were Southerners. This datum suggests that, as in the case of Southern economic grievance, relatively few Southerners formulate their complaints for themselves, but a good many are prepared to agree when someone else—a politician, a journalist, even a survey researcher—formulates one for them.

Grievance and Regional Identification

Not all Southerners share these grievances, however, and Hackney's speculation that grievance is linked to regional identification provides a lead that should be followed up. Most likely, the relation is reciprocal. Identification with a group *ought* to heighten one's sensitivity to real or imagined deprivation and slights. Likewise, believing that one's group is somehow mistreated should increase both consciousness and identification. Unfortunately, these data do not allow us to address these questions of cause and effect. But we can examine the simpler, descriptive question of whether these variables are associated with one another.

Table 5.1 shows the relation of some items designed to tap a sense of grievance to our indexes of regional identification and regional consciousness. Almost without exception, regional identification increases the likelihood that our respondents will agree that the South is being picked on and pushed around, even when those perceptions appear to be mutually contradictory (for example, when one agrees that "outsiders" both control the South and neglect it). Among those with high regional consciousness, for instance, regional identification increases by nineteen percentage points (from 40 percent to 59 percent) the likelihood that respondents will agree with the proposition that "the South could solve its problems if the rest of the country would leave it alone." Among those with low regional consciousness, identification also increases the likelihood that they will agree, by ten percentage points (from 42 percent to 52 percent).

When the proposition is reversed so that an "agree" response

*Table 5.1. Relation of Grievance Items to Regional Identification,
Controlling for Regional Consciousness*

Agree that:	Regional Consciousness					
	Low			High		
	Identification			Identification		
	Low	High	(diff.)	Low	High	(diff.)
1. Most of the things that happen in the South are the result of forces outside the South over which Southerners have little control.*	37%	42%	(5)	52%	52%	(—)
2. The South could solve its problems if the rest of the country would leave it alone.*	42%	52%	(10)	40%	59%	(19)
3. The South itself is to blame for most of its problems.**	33%	29%	(−4)	25%	20%	(−5)
4. There never would have been any progress in the South without outside assistance and pressure.	19%	18%	(−1)	17%	17%	(—)
5. The government in Washington doesn't care much what happens to the South.*	28%	26%	(−2)	25%	36%	(11)
6. The South would be a lot better off if it had won the War between the States.*	17%	24%	(7)	22%	27%	(5)
7. If it could be done without war, the South would be better off as a separate country *today*.	10%	13%	(3)	10%	12%	(2)

8. Northern industry has been making a big profit off the South's natural resources, like coal and timber, with very little return to the South.*	38%	36%	(−2)	53%	55%	(2)
9. Even if it means paying a little bit more, Southerners should take their business to locally-owned companies.	39%	47%	(8)	37%	51%	(14)
10. Most Northerners dislike Southerners.	22%	28%	(6)	28%	42%	(14)
11. Most Northerners look down on Southerners.*	40%	48%	(8)	48%	64%	(16)
12. National news programs on radio and television are nearly always unfair to the South.*	28%	27%	(−1)	27%	37%	(10)
13. Books and magazine articles about the South play up its bad points and don't give a fair picture.*	44%	47%	(3)	46%	58%	(12)
Score of 10+ on summary index (range: 0–18)	44%	47%		47%	59%	
Score of 13+ on summary index	21%	22%		25%	32%	

*Included in summary index (agree = +2, no opinion = +1, disagree = 0)
**Included in summary index (agree = 0, no opinion = +1, disagree = +2)

indicates a lack of grievance, as in "the South itself is to blame for most of its problems," identification *decreases* the likelihood of agreement. (This is reassuring, since most of the items are phrased so that "agree" means grievance, thus raising the possibility that we are measuring not grievance but "response set"— the inclination to be agreeable.)

The first six items can be taken without too much straining to indicate a sense of political efficacy or powerlessness. Several tap the belief that Southerners do not control their region's fate, that those who do have such control are unresponsive and uninterested in the South's welfare, and that greater self-determination would be desirable ("The South would be a lot better off if it had won the War Between the States").

Item 4 is particularly interesting. To disagree with the statement that "there never would have been any progress in the South without outside assistance and pressure" is to allow that the South has some control over its destiny, that it is not "a passive, insignificant object of alien or impersonal forces." On the other hand, to agree is to allow that outsiders can be beneficent. It is not at all clear how regional identification and an associated sense of grievance should affect responses; in fact, both consciousness and identification are essentially unrelated to agreement with this proposition: about 17 or 18 percent of each of the four groups in the table agreed.

Nor are the policy implications of this grievance at all straightforward. Item 7 in the table, included more or less whimsically, reveals that only a small minority, even of those with a high degree of regional identification, believe that "the South would be better off as a separate country *today*." [8] On the other hand, an-

8. This low level of support may be somewhat misleading, however. Although only 11 percent agreed with the proposition, only 74 percent disagreed; the rest were undecided and presumably had not thought about it. Even these figures are not strikingly different from the level of secessionist support in Quebec, ca. 1962, that is, before the Parti Quebecois put secession on the political agenda as a realistic option. Pinard reports that 8 percent of French-Canadians favored separation and 71 percent opposed it (*The Rise of a Third Party*, p. 81). Even in the mid-70s in Scotland, only about 20 percent of the population favored Scottish independence (Brand, *The National Movement in Scotland*, pp. 144–66).

other item (not shown in the table) reveals a rather surprising level of support (45 percent of all white respondents) for a quota system that would guarantee the South "one out of every four appointments to federal office and to the Supreme Court." Only 39 percent disapproved; the remainder were undecided.[9] In any case, many of our respondents feel a political grievance, although they disagree about what should be done about it.

Item 8 in Table 5.1 was the only one in the survey that seemed to tap an aspect of economic grievance. As we saw, Southerners do not appear to complain spontaneously about economic exploitation these days, and agreeing with this item is not related to regional identification. It is strongly related to regional *consciousness*, however, and the proportion of all respondents who agree is fairly high—a majority among those with high regional consciousness. Once again, the policy implications of this perception are unclear, but item 9 in the table offered respondents the opportunity to subscribe to a frequent nationalist response to exploitation: closing off trade with outsiders. Here a fairly large proportion of our respondents agreed with the statement, especially among those with high levels of identification.

Finally, items 11, 12, and 13 indicate a sense of *cultural* grievance, a belief that Southerners are not treated with fairness and respect by the mass media and by non-Southerners in general. Item 10 is included for comparison: notice that all categories of respondents distinguish between dislike and condescension and are more likely to perceive the latter. Both regional identification and regional consciousness increase the likelihood that Southerners will hold each of these perceptions, however, and the com-

9. Elsewhere in the survey, we included a similar question about *racial* quotas: "In a city where one-third of the people are black, some say that one out of three city employees should be black. Do you approve or disapprove of this idea?" Even making allowances for the possibility that some respondents understood the question to be asking about desirable outcomes rather than desirable policy, a good many seemed to approve of this form of quota system as well: 22 percent said it sounded like a good idea and only 42 percent rejected it outright. One reader has suggested that Southerners, accustomed for years to quotas (albeit of zero), find such schemes less ideologically objectionable than other Americans, although objection in practice may differ from objection in principle.

bination of high consciousness and high identification is particularly potent.

Although both identification and consciousness tend to be associated with various regional grievances, their patterns of association are somewhat different. We may suppose that the effects of consciousness are more constrained by the actual facts than are those of identification: increased identification means that one is more likely to agree with the sentiment behind a proposition; increased consciousness means that one's opinion about whether a statement is true or false is more likely to be a reasoned one. That at least is one explanation for the fact that identification is associated with agreeing that "the South could solve its problems if the rest of the country would leave it alone," but consciousness is not associated with it. Consciousness, on the other hand, is associated with agreeing that "most of the things that happen in the South are the result of forces outside the South over which Southerners have little control" or that "Northern industry" has been exploiting the South, but identification is not strongly associated with these items. The perception that the South is powerless is one kind of grievance, and appears to be associated with regional consciousness. Items with a more affective tone, almost regardless of their content, seem more likely to be associated with regional identification.

The summary index tabulated at the bottom of Table 5.1 shows how a generalized sense of regional grievance is related to identification and consciousness.[10] Both variables are positively associ-

---

10. Six of the nine items were found by Pamela Oliver to load highly on a dimension that she called "Southern separatism." Items 1, 2, and 6 were three of the four with the highest loadings (the other, having to do with Northern responsibility for the South's race problems, seemed too specific for inclusion here). Items 8, 12, and 13 were three of the five items with the next highest loadings (item 7 was also one of the five; however, both item 7 and item 9—further down the list—were excluded because they measured grievance less than what should be done about it). See Oliver, "Measuring Southern Separatism." The other three items in the index here are items 5 and 11 (not included in Oliver's factor analysis) and item 3. Item 3 showed a small loading on the separatism factor but a larger loading on another factor, which Oliver interpreted as an instrument factor; it picked up a number of items for which "agree" indicated the *absence* of grievance or sectional

ated with scores on this index. But each is more strongly related to grievance in the presence of the other. That is, among those with low regional consciousness, regional identification shows only a modest association with grievance. Those who do not think much in regional terms are relatively unlikely to subscribe to these complaints whether they indicate high regional identification or not. Similarly, among those with low regional identification, regional consciousness makes little difference in scores on the grievance index: if one does not identify with Southerners, simply thinking about the South is not enough to produce a sense of grievance on its behalf. But if one displays both high consciousness *and* high identification, one is quite likely indeed to believe that the South and Southerners are mistreated on a number of scores, especially, but not exclusively, in terms of dignity and respect.

Implications of a Grievance-based Identity

A sense of grievance on the South's behalf, then, is part of what it means to be a Southerner. As we have measured it, that grievance reflects a discontent with the *present* situation of the South in the nation. If regional identification depends upon this sense of grievance, rather than vice versa (a question these data do not allow us to answer), two important implications follow.

In the first place, if the South's political, economic, and cultural position continues to improve (as it undoubtedly has improved in at least the first two of these respects, even since the survey was taken) and if Southerners recognize that it has improved, regional identification may be eroded. But the process of improvement and recognition of improvement, particularly with respect to our respondents' "cultural" complaints, will presum-

---

feeling. Some of these items also appeared in the sectionalism component of Grasmick's "traditional value orientation" (in "Social Change and the Wallace Movement in the South"), although I regard them here as a *consequence* of regional identification rather than an antecedent or concomitant factor, like the rest of the traditional value orientation.

ably take some time, if it takes place at all; if it is accompanied by renewed sectional conflict, all bets are off.

The second implication of this contemporary basis for regional identification (if, to repeat, grievance is in fact a basis for identification rather than the other way around) is that it opens up the boundaries of the regional group to outsiders. It may be that one can be a Southerner if one can make the regional complaints his own. This form of identification is based on shared interests vis-à-vis outsiders, not on perceptions of cultural similarity or the possession of ascriptive "qualifications." Migrants, for example, even recent ones, can believe that what is good for the South is good for them and can resent what is seen as bad for the South. Members of minority ethnic and religious groups can do the same (and we need to know more about how and when these people regard themselves as Southerners).[11] Insofar as the grievance is not a matter of petulance about having to give up segregation, Southern blacks may well be able to make it their own, becoming in the process black Southerners. The dynamics of regional identification may be much the same for blacks and whites. That is suggested at least by the black social worker who told Sharon McKern that "in certain ways we've been more integrated here than [Northerners] have ever been. But they seem to feel superior to *all* Southerners, black and white," and by the black furniture worker who told political scientist Robert Botsch that he had voted for Jimmy Carter because he was getting tired of "listening to all these slick Yankees who think they know everything and have all the answers," and felt that he could understand and trust his fellow Southerner.[12] At present, however, we know very little about these matters.

11. See Reed, *One South*, chap. 7, "Shalom, Y'all: Southern Jews."
12. McKern, *Redneck Mothers, Good Ol' Girls, and Other Southern Belles*, and Botsch, *We Shall Not Overcome*, are quoted in a review by Vanover, "Redneck Mammas and Blue Collar Workers," pp. 27–28.

The Historical Legacy

But Southern identification is not entirely a matter of sharing the region's present grievances. In fact, to speak of "the region's grievances" may be an exaggeration: in no case did a large majority of our respondents indicate that they felt aggrieved, and even allowing for subregional differences it seems unlikely that these North Carolinians differ qualitatively from other Southerners. In any case, *present* grievances are not the whole story. Like other ethnic identities, Southern identity has its origins in history, particularly in the events leading up to the Civil War and in the war itself. In the past, the boundaries of the group have been largely defined by individuals' relation to that history. To be a Southerner was to stand in a particular relationship to the Lost Cause, to share a very specific *historical* grievance.[13] We saw in chapter 2 that ancestral loyalties still seem to be related to regional identification: many of our respondents from Unionist areas of North Carolina are still likely to be Unionists, and therefore not Southerners. And the continuing association of Southernness with the Confederacy may also be indicated by the fact that when we asked our respondents if there were any Southerners they especially admired, the most frequent response by far was Robert E. Lee, who received about one vote in five.[14]

If regional identification depends upon a conscious and literal inheritance of the Confederate tradition, however, it is in a great deal of trouble. Thirty-seven percent of our respondents were unable to tell us whether any of their ancestors fought for the Confederacy, and the percentage was substantially higher among young people than among old (although whether this documents a collective forgetting or simply an association between age and genealogical interest remains an open question). There is no association, however, between this knowledge and regional identifica-

13. See Wilson, *Baptized in Blood*, for a sensitive interpretation and exploration of this relationship as it stood at the turn of the century.

14. Tied for a distant second place were George Wallace and Billy Graham. *Sic transit gloria mundi.*

tion: 41 percent of the 285 respondents who knew of Confederate ancestors fell in the top two categories of the identification index, but so did 45 percent of the 176 who knew they did *not* have Confederate ancestors and 40 percent of the 268 who did not know whether they did or not. The relation between ancestry and regional consciousness is much the same: those who knew they had no Confederate ancestors displayed the *highest* levels of regional consciousness.

The link between attachment to the Confederacy and Southern identification may run at least as much from the identification to the attachment as vice versa. Whatever one's ancestors did (and many of our respondents did not know), it seems possible for highly identified Southerners to identify themselves with the South's history and with its historic symbols. Although the indicators in Table 5.2 are not ideal, we can use them to explore this possibility. Both identification and consciousness are associated with agreeing that "there should be more Southern history taught in our schools" and saying that one has a "great deal of interest" in Southern history. (Here the relationship to regional consciousness is particularly strong; indeed, historical interest is one thing that regional consciousness can *mean*.) Regional identification and consciousness seem to imply an interest in the regional group's history and a belief that other members of the group should be interested, or at least informed, as well.

Table 5.2 also shows the relation between consciousness and identification, on the one hand, and the attitudes toward two important Confederate symbols, the flag and the anthem, on the other. Like the statement that one is interested in Southern history, approval of the public use of "Dixie" and the Confederate flag is related to regional identification (the latter more strongly than the former, in part because almost all of these white North Carolinians liked "Dixie"). Unlike an interest in Southern history, however, these attitudes are scarcely related to regional consciousness; indeed, they are not appreciably related to an interest in Southern history, as Table 5.3 shows. Those respondents who indicate little interest in Southern history are only slightly less likely than others to approve of waving the flag and whistling

Table 5.2. Relation of Interest in Southern History and Approval of Confederate Symbolism to Regional Consciousness and Identification

	Regional Consciousness					
	Low			High		
	Identification			Identification		
	Low	High	(diff.)	Low	High	(diff.)
Agree that "there should be more Southern history taught in our schools"	53%	66%	(13)	62%	78%	(16)
Have "a great deal of interest" in Southern history	16%	26%	(10)	38%	54%	(16)
Approve of high school bands playing "Dixie" at football games	84%	86%	(2)	84%	91%	(7)
Approve of public schools displaying Confederate flag	54%	57%	(3)	49%	67%	(28)

"Dixie" in public. It seems that the song and the flag have become badges of regional identification and objects of conventional piety for many white Southerners, regardless of whether the beholder has any particular interest in the history that they represent. After all, on the "Dukes of Hazzard" television program (a sort of white Southern "Amos n' Andy"), the Duke boys had the Stars and Bars painted on the roof of their car, but no one would mistake them for students of history—or students of much of anything else, for that matter.

This is not to say that the historical connection has been wholly lost or that it is irrelevant. (The Duke boys' car *was* named "the General Lee.") For most white Southerners, the flag (if not

Table 5.3. Approval of Public Use of Confederate Symbols, by Interest in Southern History

	Score on Index of Interest in Southern History		
	Low (0–5)	Medium (6–8)	High (9–12)
Approve of high school bands playing "Dixie" at football games	83%	87%	89%
Approve of public schools displaying Confederate flag	53%	58%	58%
(N)	(185)	(335)	(193)

NOTE: Index score is summed responses to "There should be more Southern history taught in our schools" (strongly agree = +6, strongly disagree = 0) and "Would you say you have a great deal of interest in Southern history, some interest, or not much at all?" (great deal = +6; some = +3; not much, don't know = 0).

"Dixie") still *means* the Confederacy, or so one can conclude from an ingenious study by Tom Waters.[15] Waters used a picture of the Confederate battle flag as something of a projective test, asking a purposive sample of black and white North Carolinians "what comes to mind" when they see it. Thirteen of his nineteen white respondents thought of Confederate ancestors, "Rebel soldiers," or Robert E. Lee; one thought of the Ku Klux Klan; two gave idiosyncratic responses; and three said "nothing" came to mind. (Positive responses outnumbered negative ones by two to one.) Many Southern whites apparently value these symbols and value them explicitly as links with their region's past.

Many Southern blacks, of course, view those same symbols quite differently. Waters's data suggest that it is not so much that

15. Waters, "Old Times There Are Not Forgotten."

they feel differently about the Confederate legacy (although they might well do so), as that the flag and anthem symbolize to them white Southern resistance to racial equality in the more recent past. Among Waters's eleven black respondents, only one offered a Confederate association for the Confederate flag; four said they thought of racists or the Klan, and six said nothing came to mind. (Blacks are not the only Americans for whom the associations of the Confederate flag are not a matter of century-old history—or so I infer from the advertisements for biker regalia in *Easy Rider* magazine, which offer the option of the Rebel flag or the swastika.)

The opportunities for misunderstanding here are enormous, and not long ago such misunderstandings were very common. In schools throughout the South, black students protested the display of the Confederate flag and the playing of "Dixie" as insulting and demeaning to their race. In many places these practices were quietly dropped; in others whites protested that they had no such intent. As one Florida legislator put it, while seeking (successfully) to prevent local school administrators from banning "Dixie": "We're drifting away from so many of our traditions because of what people call animosities, hate inside people. Everybody's afraid they are going to hurt somebody's feelings. You know, there's no offense to anyone. It's a song of the South." [16]

If, as that quotation suggests, some white Southerners felt strongly about these symbols and were sincerely unable to understand what their associations were for black Southerners, some blacks seem either to have come to a better understanding of that point of view or simply to have decided that there are more important issues. When Governor James Hunt of North Carolina decided in 1978 to abandon the custom of flying the Confederate flag over the legislative building on Confederate Memorial Day, protest from the United Daughters of the Confederacy and other groups was strong enough that the flag was raised the next year and has been since. The governor's assistant press secretary re-

16. Quoted in Killian, *White Southerners*, p. 16.

ports that there have been no complaints, which he attributes to the fact that a great many blacks are now in state government—not really a non sequitur, perhaps.[17]

In any case, insofar as Southern identity is linked to the Confederate heritage, it would seem almost necessarily to be racially exclusive (although the number of black athletes and cheerleaders who play and cheer for teams called the "Rebels" is startling). It strikes me as remarkable that Southern blacks are willing to tolerate their white neighbors' nostalgia on that score, and it seems altogether too much to expect them to subscribe to it. Clearly, however, the legacy of the Confederacy and its linkage with regional identity is not what it used to be. Table 5.4 shows that even their statistical association is modest. The Confederate heritage has been "put in perspective." Virginia's legislators recently added a remembrance of Martin Luther King to the Old Domin-

Table 5.4. Regional Identification, by Support for Confederate Symbols

Identification	Score on Index of Support for Confederate Symbols†		
	Low (0–6)	Medium (9)	High (12)
High 6	18%	15%	25%
5	19	25	21
4	31	29	31
3	13	8	10
Low 0–2	18	24	14
Total	99%*	101%*	101%*
(N)	(223)	(120)	(386)

*Total differs from 100% due to rounding error.
†Summed responses to questions concerning public use of Confederate flag and "Dixie": approve = 6; don't know, depends = 3; disapprove = 0.

17. Waters, "Old Times There Are Not Forgotten," pp. 6–7.

ion's traditional Lee-Jackson Day (apparently with the idea that citizens can now celebrate whatever they feel like celebrating). And the last straw may be the "Monster Plantation" in the Confederate section of the Six Flags over Georgia park, where visitors are greeted by some 130 animated creatures, including Mizzy Scarlett (the hostess) and Billy Bob Fritter. It is described by the park's Director of Corporate Public Relations as "the latest state-of-the-art in three-dimensional dark rides."

Roots of Identification in the Past and Present

We have examined two correlates of regional identification among Southerners: a sense of grievance concerning the South's present situation—economic, political, and cultural—within the United States and an identification—sometimes ancestral but apparently often assumed—with the region's history and the historic symbols

Table 5.5. Grievance Index, by Index of Interest in Southern History

		Low (0–5)	Medium (6–8)	High (9–12)
		Score on Index of Interest in Southern History†		
Score on Grievance Index		Low (0–5)	Medium (6–8)	High (9–12)
High	(13–18)	21%	28%	36%
	(10–12)	18	22	23
	(5–9)	31	30	26
Low	(0–4)	30	19	14
Total		100%	99%*	99%*
(N)		(185)	(335)	(193)

*Total differs from 100% due to rounding error.
†See Table 5.3.

of the Confederacy. Obviously the two are not mutually exclusive: Table 5.5 shows that those with the greatest interest in the South's history are the most likely to share the regional grievances and vice versa, although a sense of regional grievance does *not* seem to be associated with support for the symbols of the Confederacy (see Table 5.6).

We cannot say that regional identification is a product of history *or* that it is, like social class, linked to present condition. As with most ethnic identities, both work, to different extents for different people. In Table 5.7 I have displayed the joint effects of the two on identification. (The index of historical identification is simply a combination of support for Confederate symbols and interest in Southern history.)[18] Table 5.7 suggests that, should old times there ever be forgotten, current grievances can serve to bolster

Table 5.6. Grievance Index, by Index of Support for Confederate Symbols

		Score on Index of Support for Confederate Symbols*		
Score on Grievance Index		Low (0–6)	Medium (9)	High (12)
High	(13–18)	32%	34%	27%
	(10–12)	20	19	22
	(5–9)	29	29	29
Low	(0–4)	19	18	22
Total		100%	100%	100%
(N)		(229)	(120)	(391)

*See Table 5.4.

18. When related to regional identification and the grievance index, both the index of interest in Southern history and the index of support for Confederate symbols behave in much the same way as their sum, the index of historical identification. I have chosen to present merely that sum here.

Table 5.7. *Regional Identification, by Grievance Index and Index
of Historical Identification*

| | Percentage High Regional Identification (5–6) (N) | | | |
| | Score on Index of Historical Identification* | | | |
Score on Grievance Index	Low (0–14)	(15–19)	(20)	High (21+)
High (13–18)	39% (56)	44% (72)	50% (36)	73% (37)
Low (0–13)	29% (157)	35% (205)	53% (70)	56% (75)

*Sum of indexes of interest in Southern history (table 5.3) and support for
Confederate symbols (table 5.4).

regional identification. In the unlikely event that current grievances are done away with, the historical facts will serve.

It is dangerous, of course, to adopt the language of causality. In
Table 5.7 we do not know what is cause and what effect or, for
that matter, whether all three variables are not effects of some
other unmeasured cause. But whether one shares regional grievances or not, an interest in the South's history and an attachment
to the symbols of the Lost Cause seem to be generally associated
with increased regional identification. Similarly, regardless of the
level of historical identification, a sense of grievance on the
South's behalf is associated with increased identification. If both
are present, identification is especially likely to be found: 71 percent of those who score high on both indexes display high regional identification.

But the implications of present grievance and historical pride
are quite different. To the extent that regional identification is

linked to the past, in particular to the Confederate heritage, whether in actual genealogical fact or through a belated pledge of allegiance to the Stars and Bars, the circle of "Southerners" will be closed to many potential recruits—to Southern blacks, to many whites in the Southern mountains, and to many migrants. On the other hand, seeing the South as mistreated is a correlate not only of regional identification but of regional consciousness: that perception is open to anyone who wants to think about American regional relations and evidently can produce regional identification as well.

"Would You Want Your Daughter. . . ?"

Prejudice, Social Distance, and Boundary Maintenance

By this point, it should be clear that regional groups are social and psychological facts. They exist in people's minds and serve to order individuals' perceptions of others. Many of our respondents believe that there are important differences between Northerners and Southerners and report that they feel closer to other Southerners. When forced to choose, many chose a Southerner (thereby rejecting a non-Southerner) for a hypothetical job and in a hypothetical election. But so far we have not looked directly at the nastier side of intergroup relations, at prejudice and discrimination, hostility toward the out-group, ethnocentrism. In particular, we have not looked at whether the attitudes we have been studying have any effect on actual behavior, on the patterns of association and avoidance that social psychologists have studied under the label of "social distance."[1]

---

1. The "social distance" metaphor was introduced by Robert Park in his 1924 article, "The Concept of Social Distance," but the phrase has come to be associated with the work of E. S. Bogardus, who devised the most commonly used scale

Let us look first at the relevant attitudes. In chapter 3 we saw that a good many Southerners hold stereotypes of their own group and also of the regional out-group, Northerners, which provides a context for "Southerners" and largely gives that concept its meaning. These stereotypes are well defined and widely shared. They seem in part to reflect actual experience with regional differences. Most important, they are not wholly unflattering to Northerners or favorable toward Southerners. Our index of stereotyping, in other words, does not measure what we usually think of as "prejudice," if by that we mean hostility, fear, or suspicion of the out-group. These affective components of one's regional attitudes are tapped more directly by our identification measures, although even with those we are measuring less how one feels about Northerners than how one feels about Southerners.[2] To the extent that Southern identification carries with it a sense of grievance toward the North and to the extent that individual Southerners fail to distinguish between a sectional grievance against the North and a personal grievance against Northerners, we may have tapped regional prejudice with those items, but the inferential chain is a little long and a little weak.

Sectional Prejudice and Regional Stereotyping

The survey unfortunately did not contain very good measures of sectional hostility, but three items can be combined into an index that captures several aspects of anti-Northern prejudice. The three "agree-disagree" items are: (1) "I don't like to hear a person with a Northern accent"; (2) "Marriages between Northerners and Southerners are just as happy as marriages where both people

---

for measuring it. For a review, see Harding et al., "Prejudice and Ethnic Relations." For a general discussion of the affective, cognitive, and behavioral components of attitudes, see Triandis, *Attitude and Attitude Change*, pp. 60–100. Some interesting recent European work is included in a review by David Milner, "Racial Prejudice," in Turner and Giles, *Intergroup Behavior*.

2. Lewin would say that we have measured the "valence" of the in-group, Southerners, but not that of the out-group—that is, pull, but not push.

come from the same part of the country" (scored negatively); and (3) "People who move to the South from the North never really become Southerners."[3] Saying that Northerners sound unpleasant, that Southerners who marry them will be sorry, and that they are unassimilable would seem, on the face of it, to be fairly valid indicators of prejudice.

The relationship between this index and the measure of regional stereotyping from chapter 3 is an interesting one. The two indexes are essentially uncorrelated (tau-b = .03). Some of the individual items in the stereotyping index *are* associated with prejudice toward Northerners, both positively and negatively. The belief that they are less loyal to their families, for instance, is positively associated with prejudice, as measured here; the belief that they are more industrious is negatively associated with prejudice. But a number of the items, including the belief that Southerners are slower, more courteous, less materialistic, or less so phisticated, are not correlated at all with prejudice, and neither is the composite index. Live and let live, apparently.

In large measure, however, it appears that stereotyping and prejudice are not correlated because their antecedents are quite different—opposite, in fact. We saw in chapter 3 that exposure to non-Southerners was positively associated with holding the conventional regional stereotypes (up to a point, at least). As Figure 6.1 shows, exposure to non-Southerners strongly and consistently reduces the prejudice toward them. Education (which increases the propensity to stereotype) also reduces anti-Northern prejudice among Southerners.

The absence of an association between stereotyping and prejudice does not mean that one does not affect the other (if anything, the evidence is to the contrary, especially with education, exposure, and so forth held constant). Rather, the same sorts of experiences and conditions that lead Southerners to stereotype non-Southerners act to reduce sectional prejudice and animosity;

3. Details of the construction of this index and an analysis of its correlates (which includes most of that presented here) can be found in Reed, *One South*, chap. 6, "Getting to Know You."

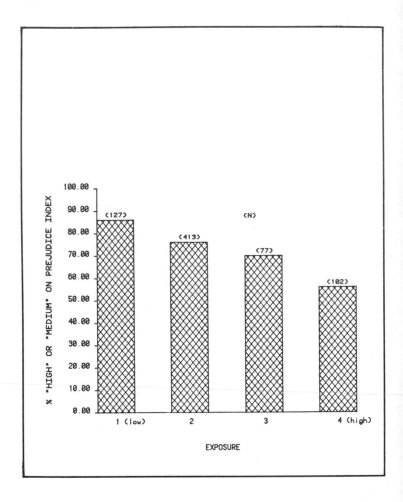

Figure 6.1. Relation of Anti-Northern Prejudice to Exposure

SOURCE: John Shelton Reed, "Getting to Know You: The Contact Hypothesis Applied to the Sectional Beliefs and Attitudes of White Southerners," *Social Forces* 59, no. 1 (September 1980): 133, fig. 2.

NOTE: See Figure 3.1 for definition of exposure variable.

the types of Southerners who are likely to dislike non-Southerners are the same types who are unlikely to know (or even to think they know) much about them. This is similar to the situation described in chapter 3, where education, urban residence, and exposure to non-Southerners—the whole range of modernizing experiences—lead Southerners to be aware of their regional affiliation, at the same time reducing the likelihood that they will subscribe to the traditional value orientation. Stereotyping is related, both empirically and conceptually, to regional consciousness. Just so, anti-Northern prejudice may be related to the traditional value orientation. Harold Grasmick's data suggest this; moreover, much of the traditional value orientation concerns drawing firm lines between categories—racial and religious groups, the sexes, those inside and outside one's family or local community—and distrusting outsiders of all sorts.[4] As *regional* outsiders, non-Southerners come in for their share of this suspicion and hostility from the more traditional elements of the Southern population.

Social Distance, South to North

Compared to other animosities, however, sectional ill will is apparently at a fairly low level. Although considerable fractions of our sample agreed with each of the statements that we used to measure prejudice against non-Southerners (that Northern accents are unattractive, that regional intermarriage can lead to difficulty, and that the boundaries between regional groups are relatively impermeable), it would be wrong to say that sectional prejudice is substantial or widespread. When we ask whether these attitudes have any implications for actual behavior, when we turn to the "conative" aspects of regional attitudes, we find surprisingly little. Our measure of identification indicates that many respondents would choose a Southerner over a Northerner if they were forced to pick one or the other, but in less symmetric situations, where

4. Grasmick, "Social Change and the Wallace Movement in the South."

discrimination would be spontaneous rather than forced, we find little disposition to engage in it.

The usual way to measure the conative aspect of intergroup attitudes is with an index of "social distance." Members of one group are asked whether they would be willing to admit members of another group to increasingly intimate association—to work at the same job, to live on the same block, to go to the same party, to entertain at home, to have as a close relative by marriage. In most applications, as the association becomes more intimate, smaller proportions say they would tolerate it.[5] This measure is of course secondhand: it does not examine the extent to which members of the out-group actually *are* admitted to various sorts of association but rather the extent to which in-group members say they are willing to admit them. This has obvious shortcomings, but so do measures of actual association. Most Southerners work with other Southerners, live in neighborhoods with them, marry them. But this would be the case in any event; propinquity alone insures as much, and observing it tells us nothing at all about whether regional attitudes actually affect people's behavior.

The "bottom line" of the social distance scale boils down to a paraphrase of the old Southern question, "Would you want your daughter to marry one?" In this survey, we began at the end, with this question: "Suppose you had a daughter who wants to marry a young man who was born and raised in the North, but lives here now. Would the fact that he was from the North make you feel good about him, feel bad about him, or wouldn't it make any difference?" (The stipulation "but lives here now" was intended to isolate the background component from the residential one. Since some of the respondents who objected said they did so because they did not want their hypothetical daughter to leave the area, this manipulation seems not to have worked in some cases.)

This seems an obvious item to have included in the index of regional prejudice; it was not included because there is very little variation in the responses it elicited. Nearly all of our respondents said that the young man's origins would not make any difference

5. See Harding et al., "Prejudice and Ethnic Relations."

to them (and some of those who said they would make a difference seem to have misunderstood the question). Although objecting to the marriage shows a slight relationship to identification, as Table 6.1 shows, even among those with the highest levels of identification—those who feel closer to other Southerners and would hire a Southern scientist and vote for a Southern congressman, other things equal—only 3 percent would "feel bad" about a Northern son-in-law and 92 percent say it would make no difference. Presumably they would prefer a Southern son-in-law, but not so strongly that they would "feel bad" about a Northern one. Only a handful said they would "feel good" about it (and most of those were transplanted Northerners themselves), but the vast majority were tolerant or at least indifferent, suggesting that social distance based on region is of a lower order of magnitude in the United States than that based on race or religion.

In addition, this item's negligible association with our index of identification supports the interpretation that regional identification has less to do with feelings toward Northerners than with feelings toward fellow Southerners. Apparently, "social space" is

Table 6.1. Feelings about a Northern Son-in-Law, by Level of Regional Identification

	Regional Identification				
	Low 0–2	3	4	5	High 6
Would feel good about him	2%	1%	1%	—%	—%
Would feel bad about him	—	1	3	1	3
Would make no difference	95	96	95	97	93
It depends	2	1	1	2	4
Total	99%*	101%*	100%	100%	100%
(N)	(120)	(75)	(219)	(151)	(150)

*Total differs from 100% due to rounding error. Response "don't know" is excluded.

not like physical space: feeling "close" to one's own group does not necessarily mean feeling "distant" from the out-group.[6]

But guesses about how one would feel or act in a hypothetical situation are rather indirect measures of the actual effects of regional group membership on patterns of association and avoidance. If we could find a situation where both Southerners and non-Southerners are present, we could examine the patterns of interaction and friendship, and see whether in-group choices are more frequent than we would expect to occur by chance, whether, in other words, there is regional "homophily."[7]

Regional Homophily at a Southern University

There is an extensive body of research on background factors influencing interaction of various sorts, but unfortunately I could find no data that recorded the regional origins of the participants.[8] In the apparent absence of any existing data on the subject, I conducted a small-scale sample survey of undergraduates at the University of North Carolina, Chapel Hill, in 1976.[9] It is difficult

6. See, for instance, Lipscomb, "Parental Influence in the Development of Black Children's Racial Self-Esteem"; Williams and Morland, *Race, Color, and the Young Child*.

7. The term is Robert Merton's, from Lazarsfeld and Merton, "Friendship as a Social Process." For a discussion of how it might be measured, see Coleman, "Relational Analysis," and for an example of the sort of inquiry that is needed (although focusing on religious groups rather than regional ones), see Caplovitz and Levy, "Inter-religious Dating among College Students."

8. One promising lead was found in Janowitz, *The Professional Soldier*, p. 204, which cites an unpublished research report to the effect that regional origin was a principal basis for clique formation on a Southern Air Force base. That report (Simpson, "Friendship Cliques in the United States Air Force Wings") is now unavailable, but its author recalls that he merely cited in turn another unpublished report, by an anthropologist who reported his impression that Southerners and "Yankees" formed distinct friendship groups on the base.

9. The survey was conducted by mail questionnaire to a systematic sample of undergraduates listed in the official student directory and yielded a return rate of roughly 85 percent with one follow-up. The data are available from the data library of the Institute for Research in Social Science, the University of North Carolina, Chapel Hill.

to say to what extent the findings from this sample are generalizable to other populations in other settings, although the same difficulty would be encountered for studies of military bases, resorts, metropolitan areas, company towns, or any other setting that brings together people from different regions. Perhaps college students are less inclined than older or less well-educated people to choose friends who resemble themselves, or perhaps my stereotype of college students is too flattering. Nonetheless, these data do reveal some degree of regional homophily, particularly among the non-Southern students, who are a decided minority in the Chapel Hill setting.

We asked each respondent to list, by initials, his three best friends at the university and to answer a number of questions about them. One of the questions was how many of the three were from the South. Close to 90 percent of the students in Chapel Hill are from the South (the precise figure depends both on how "the South" is defined and on what it means to be "from" somewhere). So if students chose their friends without regard for where they came from, we would expect only a fraction of 1 percent to have no Southerners among their three best friends; about 4 percent to have only one; about 28 percent to choose two Southerners out of the three; and the majority, over two-thirds, to have no non-Southern friends at all. This would simply reflect the composition of the pool from which friends *could* be chosen, not Southern ethnocentrism.

Table 6.2 shows the deviations from this pattern. Non-Southern students were much more likely than chance would predict to say that none or only one of their best friends was from the South and much less likely to say that all three were. Overall, non-Southern students reported that about a third of their best friends were also non-Southerners, a percentage roughly three times what random selection of friends would lead us to predict.[10] Southern students,

10. One plausible alternative hypothesis—that the relevant distinction is not between Southern and non-Southern students but between in-state students (who are likely to retain some friendships from high school) and out-of-state students (who are more stringently selected and come from a somewhat "alien" background)—is not supported by the data. In this respect, Southern out-of-state students resemble those from North Carolina, not other students from out of the state.

Table 6.2. Number of "Three Best Friends" from the South, for Southern and Non-Southern University Students

Number of Friends from South	Expected Percentage (assuming random choice of friends)	Southern Students	Non-Southern Students
None	—%*	3%	9%
One	4	5	19
Two	28	21	33
Three	68	71	39
	100%	100%	100%
(N)		(545)	(64)

*Less than one-half of 1%.

on home ground, were less likely to seek each other out: their friends' regional backgrounds conformed fairly closely to the overall population distribution and, if anything, they were as likely to have "too many" non-Southern friends (given the composition of the pool) as "too few."

Table 6.3 provides more detail. Given the lopsided preponderance of Southerners and the fact that students living in dormitories have little to say about whom they live with, it is impressive that even 17 percent of the non-Southern students have contrived to find living quarters where a majority of their coresidents are also non-Southerners. In contexts where association is more voluntary, the proportion of non-Southerners who associate mostly with other non-Southerners increases: 28 percent "go out" mostly with other non-Southerners; 31 percent say most of their close friends are non-Southerners (a figure close to what we would estimate from Table 6.2); a third of those who date date mostly non-Southerners; and 46 percent of the non-Southern students who answered the question said they intended to marry a non-Southerner. Notice that we have here the usual pattern for social distance items: as the association becomes more intimate, the proportion who restrict it to members of their own group increases.

Table 6.3. Regional Homophily in Choice of Associates, for Southern and Non-Southern University Students

Context	Percentage Reporting More than Half of Associates from Regional In-group	
	Southern Students	Non-Southern Students
Among those in same living group	89%	17%
Among those respondent "goes out with" (regardless of sex)	89%	28%
Among close friends ("those you could confide in")	87%	31%
Among those respondent dates*	84%	33%
Percentage who expect to marry within group**	92%	46%

*Excludes 11% of Southerners and 12% of non-Southerners who do not date.
**Excludes 56% of Southerners and 60% of non-Southerners who do not know.
Married students indicated spouses' backgrounds.

In all of the situations we asked about, the vast majority of Southern students reported that they interacted primarily with other Southerners—a hardly surprising fact, given the composition of the population. It may be that Southern students are slightly *more* likely to date non-Southerners than chance would lead us to expect, but those who are thinking of marriage "overchoose" Southerners somewhat. These data, while suggestive, leave several interesting questions unanswered. They strengthen the supposition that although regional *attitudes* may be important psychological facts, Southerners in the South seldom translate them into discriminatory *behavior* toward non-Southerners. On the other hand, for the non-Southern students in our sample, what region someone comes from appears to be an important datum in organizing (consciously or unconsciously) one's association with him.

Why do the non-Southern students appear more ethnocentric than the Southern ones? There are two possible interpretations, and our data do not allow us to choose between them. On the one hand, they could *be* more ethnocentric: those North Carolinians who told us that "most Northerners look down on Southerners" could be right, and the social distance from Northerner to Southerner could be greater than the distance going in the opposite direction. If true, this would replicate the usual finding of research on intergroup relations, that dominant groups express more distance from subordinate groups than vice versa, assuming that Southerners can be regarded as the subordinate group in this case.[11] We simply do not know enough about the regional attitudes of *non*-Southerners to be able to say. On the other hand, non-Southern students at North Carolina are self-selected to begin with: they presumably did not feel *too* much social distance from Southerners or they would have gone to college somewhere else.

It seems more likely to me that we are seeing simply the obverse of what we observed in chapter 3 among Southerners who had spent time in the North, namely, the heightening of regional consciousness by the experience of living in a setting outside one's native region. Certainly, as Table 6.4 shows, these non-Southern students are somewhat more likely than their Southern classmates to believe that there are regional differences in values, goals, and interests, and we have seen earlier that such a belief is correlated with heightened regional consciousness.

Perhaps we can generalize. A situation where one's group exists as a very small minority in relation to another, where the larger group is seen as "normal" (and the smaller, by implication at least, as "alien"), must be asymmetric in its effects. The function of social distance is to maintain group boundaries, and the

11. Reed, *The Enduring South*, p. 22, presents data from a 1957 Gallup poll, showing that anti-Southern sentiment was then somewhat more common among non-Southerners than anti-Northern feeling among Southerners.

Table 6.4. Perception of Regional Differences in Values, Goals, and Interests, among Southern and Non-Southern University Students

See:	Southern Students	Non-Southern Students
Major differences	14%	27%
Slight differences	51	56
No differences	32	22
Don't know	3	—
	100%	100%
(N)	(543)	(64)

boundaries of the smaller group are threatened in a way that those of the majority group are not, particularly if those who cross group boundaries are seen as assimilable to the new group. There is no danger that Southern students in Chapel Hill will cease to be Southern, but non-Southern students might well go native. Some do.

The fact of being a minority is itself sufficient to sensitize group members to their status and to cause them to seek each other out for support and comfort. But when the setting *threatens* members' group identity, that tendency may be exacerbated. Examples from the experience of other groups in American society come readily to mind. On the other hand, in situations like this one, where there is no serious prejudice against the minority group, where no one minds if his daughter marries one, where even the possibility of group membership is open to outsiders, members of the majority group will be more likely—because they can *afford* it—just to take others as they come.

CHAPTER 7

The End of the Beginning

The time has come to gather up the threads of this narrative, to impose some order on these findings, to summarize them, and to venture some conclusions. Making every allowance for the inadequacies of the data, for peculiar and unrepresentative samples, and for measurement that is often less persuasive than one might wish, it is still clear that we can reject one simple and (to some) appealing view of what is happening to Southerners in the closing years of the twentieth century. The economic and demographic changes that have swept across the region have clearly *not* rendered Southern identity useless and irrelevant, nor have they doomed it to early extinction.

To be sure, these changes have had momentous consequences for Southerners: not just for their standard of living and for the settings in which they make and do that living, but for the South's culture, for its politics, its patterns of race relations and family life, the nature of its towns and cities, and much else besides. Some of these changes, nearly everyone would agree, have been improvements; others, in my view at least, have been regrettable; perhaps most have simply been changes. But, for better or for worse, Southerners are becoming more "modern"—that is to say, more "American"—in many respects, particularly those that are linked to urban life, education, and exposure to the "outside world."

The question of regional differences may be another matter. In certain areas, limits to this process of change may preserve some residual differences between the South and the rest of the United States; in others, the South may be aiming at a moving target; in still other areas—in some aspects of religion and politics, for example—the South does not seem to be changing at all or seems to be changing *away* from the national norm.[1]

In one respect, however, there seems little question that regional differences are evaporating: the traditional value orientation that has served as an ethnic marker, distinguishing Southerners, in the aggregate, from other Americans, is on the wane. I once saw one of those sappy posters, probably mass-produced in California, with a yellow "Happy Face" and the legend "Today is the first day of the rest of your life." Some philosopher had altered it to read "Today is the last day of the first part of your life." This elegiac posture may be a characteristically Southern stance, but the revised statement is certainly as accurate. As new things begin, old ones end. Southernness as we have known it is almost over. It seems to have a future, but in some new form, as yet indistinct.

Perhaps, in some sense, the regional differences that are going away are "the important ones" and may somehow *count* more than the ones that remain. Certainly those—on both political right and left—who feel that racism is central to Southern culture will find the decreasing differences in that respect of tremendous and perhaps decisive importance. But that judgment is imposed from outside: most Southerners do not regard the "Southern way of life" as identical with or even particularly dependent on racial oppression. (Although 21 percent of our sample agreed that "the best thing about the Southern way of life was racial segregation," 64 percent disagreed, most of them vehemently.) As we saw in chapter 3, most people talked about manners, friendliness, morality, style, and "pace" when we asked about important regional differences.[2]

1. For a general discussion of the issues involved in "assimilation," see Abramson, "Assimilation and Pluralism."

2. Lyman and Douglass wisely allude to the "certain sense of ineffableness with which members define the boundaries of their group" ("Ethnicity," p. 346). See also the distinction proposed by Royce between ethnic *tradition* and ethnic

In short, although the content of Southernness is changing, it still is believed to have some content. Moreover, the other, persistent differences between Southerners and other Americans imply that regional categories will remain a useful way to organize the data of experience, not just for survey researchers (who always include region as a "face-sheet datum") but for ordinary Americans who have occasion to interact with people from different regions.[3] Even if this were not the case, of course, regional concepts and regional stereotypes could be widely held, perpetuated by folklore, the educational system, and the mass media.[4] As long as *non-Southerners* think of Southerners as "different"—whether because they *are* different or because non-Southerners have learned to think that way for some other reason—Southerners, our data suggest, will be pushed to think in those terms as well.

From the group's standpoint, and from my rather different one, the important differences are those (whatever they may be) that mark the group's boundaries, those that people *believe* are important. For any ethnic group, these are the critical differences. They are subject to change and some may even be fictitious, but as long as people believe that they set the group off from outsiders, the distinction between in-group and out-group will order people's thoughts, structure their behavior, and contribute to their identity.[5]

As the anthropologist Fredrik Barth has put it, "The critical focus of investigation [in research on ethnicity is] the ethnic *boundary* that defines the group, not the cultural stuff that it en-

---

style (Ethnic Identity, pp. 9–15, 147). Gans suggests one possible outcome in "Symbolic Ethnicity."

3. Ethnic identities and stereotypes can have uses other than cognitive, as Lyman and Douglass, among others, have observed (see "Ethnicity").

4. "An ethnic identity . . . becomes a personal identity after an individual appropriates it from a cultural source, that is, from the public display and traffic in symbols" (Keyes, "The Dialectics of Ethnic Change," p. 10). Gans emphasizes the importance of the mass media in defining and diffusing the symbols of ethnicity in the present-day United States ("Symbolic Ethnicity," p. 12).

5. For related discussions, see, for instance, Keyes, "The Dialectics of Ethnic Change," p. 7, or Royce, *Ethnic Identity*, p. 12.

closes." He observes that "the fact of continuing dichotomization between members and outsiders" can remain even though the "cultural features that signal the boundary may change and the cultural characteristics of the members may likewise be transformed"; that boundaries can remain boundaries "despite what may figuratively be called the 'osmosis' of personnel through them"; and that "a drastic reduction of cultural differences between ethnic groups does not correlate in any simple way with a reduction in the organizational relevance of ethnic identities, or a breakdown in boundary-maintaining processes." [6]

Barth's point of view implies that ethnic identity will be most salient at the group's boundary, recalling the paradox that underlies the confusing relationships among the variables that we have studied here. It is not those Southerners whose cognitive horizons are most constricted, not those most isolated from the American mainstream, who will find their regional identity most salient. Rather it is those who are most modern in background and experience—the increasing proportion of Southerners who live in cities, who have had a good deal of education, who travel and watch television and read, who do business with non-Southerners—who (if they are not lost to the regional group altogether) are most likely to think in regional terms, to categorize themselves and others as "Southerners" and "non-Southerners," and to believe that they know what that means.

Thus regional identification, a feeling of closeness to other Southerners and of community with them, may be threatened by the cultural changes that are making Southerners more like other Americans, but it is sustained by the fact that increasing numbers of Southerners have backgrounds and experiences that make that identification relevant to them. The fact that identification is not

6. See Barth, *Ethnic Groups and Boundaries*, pp. 9–38; the quotations are from pp. 15, 14, 21, and 32–33. Barth also remarks that "overt, 'objective' differences" may not be the socially relevant *differentiae* (p. 15) and that perhaps "the sharing of a common culture" should be regarded "as an implication or result, rather than a primary and definitional characteristic of ethnic group organization" (p. 11). Barth's view is simply assumed in much recent work on ethnicity, including most of those works cited above.

statistically associated to any great degree with the various "modernizing" variables we examined does not mean that these variables have nothing to do with identification; it means, rather, that they operate through two different mechanisms, both to increase it and to decrease it. Similarly, stereotyping of non-Southerners and prejudice against them are not associated because stereotyping (like regional consciousness, to which it is closely related) is increased by real or vicarious experiences with outsiders, but prejudice against them (closely linked to the traditional value orientation and its component of general ethnocentrism) is decreased by these same experiences.

Identification as a Southerner carries with it a good deal of emotional and cognitive freight, especially in the form of various grievances against the North and attachment to the historic symbols of the South, but it is more a correlate of sectional hostility than a cause of it. The latter can decrease, and it almost certainly is decreasing, without directly affecting regional identification.

So, at the end, we return to a general proposition: categories become groups, entities that enlist the loyalties and affect the self-definitions of their members, through their relations with other groups. Questions of identity are brought to consciousness for us, attributes become part of our selves, when we encounter others who are different, or who insist that we are different. Group membership is most salient at the social and cultural periphery of a group; at its core, other aspects of identity take precedence. In the United States in this century, the conditions of life increasingly put Southerners (and members of other "primordial" groups as well) "at the periphery," willy-nilly; these conditions increasingly pose the question, "Who are you?"—the answer to which, in other times and places, may have gone without saying. For some—for many, it appears—"a Southerner" is part of the answer.

This general observation is not a new one. Andrew Greeley has stated it perhaps most clearly and forcefully in an extended critique of the assimilationist assumptions that have underpinned much of American scholarship on ethnicity. He quotes Ilona Fabian: "People, while living in their own society, take their culture and identity to a great extent for granted. . . . [Q]uestions of cultural identity arise only when immigrants are asked by the host society, 'Who are you?'. . . . [T]he self-identification of the immigrant is not merely a reflection upon the old culture, [it is] also a response to a question posed by the host society in terms of its own categories."[7] Anyone who wants to understand Southern identity and what is happening to it in these last years of the twentieth century should read Greeley's work on American ethnicity, Harold Isaacs on "basic group identity," and Clifford Geertz on "primordial attachments."[8]

The sort of thing I am saying about Southerners is no longer particularly novel. Other people have been saying similar things about other groups in recent years. Why, then, are people reluctant to accept the logic of this argument when it is applied to American regional groups, in particular to Southerners?[9] At the risk of sounding aggrieved, I will venture to suggest that there may be an element of wishful thinking in their unwillingness to accept this argument, an element most evident when outsiders betray their assumption that this tiresome business of Southern exceptionalism will soon be gone with the wind. And, to be fair, I should add that some natives have also looked forward with relief to the time when they could lay down the burden of Southern identity.

Apparently, however, Southernness still remains important, in some ways more important than ever. The South's "confrontation with mass society," as Alvin Bertrand called it, has indeed

7. Greeley, *Ethnicity in the United States*, especially pp. 2–33 and 291–323. The quotation, from an unpublished research proposal, is on pp. 301–2. Royce cites Abner Cohen on "retribalization" in Africa, which occurs precisely *because* of increasing interaction between groups (*Ethnic Identity*, p. 168).

8. See, for example, Isaacs, *Idols of the Tribe*; Geertz, "The Integrated Revolution."

9. Greeley is an exception. In *Ethnicity in the United States*, he devotes a chapter (pp. 253–70) to the subject of regional variation in the culture of white Protestants and concludes that "regional . . . diversity among American Protestants may play a quasi-ethnic role" (p. 270). Another exception is a journalist, Joel Garreau, who has recently argued for the continued—perhaps renewed—importance of regions in American life (*The Nine Nations of North America*).

altered the region, in ways that were long ago predicted. But that confrontation has not reached the "final stage of more or less complete surrender" to mass society.[10] Despite mass society, Southerners are and apparently will remain "different"; *because* of it (this analysis leads me to believe), they will remain aware of their difference. By doing so, however, they are no different—no different from the other cultural minorities that make up late twentieth-century American society.

10. Bertrand, "The Emerging Rural South," p. 457.

APPENDIX A

The Survey of North Carolina

Angell G. Beza

The sample design for the "Survey of North Carolina" had a dual purpose: to establish a framework for the selection of a representative sample of households throughout the state for the survey itself and to serve as the basis for other statewide surveys. Indeed, before the "Survey of North Carolina" was conducted in 1971, a survey of crime victimization was fielded. In following years, the same basic sample design was used to conduct a study of outdoor recreational practices and needs and a study of the social and economic well-being of the aged in the state.

The "Survey of North Carolina" itself included multiple studies. In addition to the study reported here, the survey included a number of topical issues common to public opinion polling, an "omnibus" section that accommodated social science faculty interests ranging from basic patterns of population migration to the public agenda-setting function of the media, and a study of the subjective well-being of North Carolinians.

The dual purpose of the sample design and the multiple studies included in the survey required a set of procedures that would allow approximately twelve hundred households in any of the surveys to represent the entire state. To be representative, the sample had to include the major regions of the state and the settlement patterns of the population within those regions. Fortunately, North Carolina has three distinctive natural regions in which differences in terrain and geographical location have led to differences in agricultural and industrial development and thus to differences in settlement patterns. Each of these regions—the mountains, piedmont, and coastal plain—was first delineated as a separate geographical area from which a sample of households would be drawn. To take further account of geographical diversity and thereby to capture potential differences in people and their way of life, the two larger regions were subdivided. Thus, five geographical regions of the state were delineated, each with about an equal share of the state's 100 counties: mountains (17 counties), northern piedmont (18), southern piedmont (20), northern coastal plain (28), and southern coastal plain (17).

Another striking feature of North Carolina, especially in 1970, was its diversity of human settlements. Slightly more than half of the population lived in rural areas or open country (defined as areas with fewer than twenty-five hundred inhabitants). The other half of the population was about evenly divided between cities with fifty thousand or more inhabitants and the remaining areas, which fell between clearly rural areas and urban areas (small towns and small cities). Since the urban way of life often extends beyond the city limits, densely populated areas around the major cities were included as urbanized areas. Each of the major urban areas in the state was included in the sample design.

The five regions of the state and the three types of population settlements comprised the overall design of the sample. The resulting fourteen strata (the northern coastal plain did not contain an urbanized area) are shown in Table A.1.

It was estimated that most of the surveys using this sample design would include approximately twelve hundred household interviews. Ideally, these households would be scattered throughout North Carolina. But the costs of interviewer travel time and distance usually result in some degree of clustering in household

Table A.1. Distribution of 120 Sample Points for North Carolina

	Mountains	Northern Piedmont	Southern Piedmont	Northern Coastal Plain	Southern Coastal Plain	Total
Urbanized Areas	2	15	7	0	5	29
Other Urban Areas	1	4	9	7	4	25
Rural Areas	7	15	18	13	13	66
Totals	10	34	34	20	22	120

surveys. Although clustering reduces costs, it runs the risk of including households that are very similar to each other because of their close proximity. Balancing these opposing considerations resulted in a cluster size of ten households. Thus, clusters of ten households from each of the 120 sample points indicated in Table A.1 would yield the desired sample size of twelve hundred. The number of sample points in each stratum in Table A.1 proportionately reflects the total population of North Carolina in 1970.

Selecting the sample for the "Survey of North Carolina" involved three steps: transforming the overall sample design of fourteen strata into specific geographical areas of the state, selecting 120 clusters of households within these strata, and choosing one adult from each household to be interviewed. The first step was performed with information from the 1970 Census of Population and Housing in a form available only on computer tapes. The most detailed information made available to the public were units of persons and households known as census enumeration districts in rural areas and block-groups in urban areas. Each of these units contained approximately 250 households and eight hundred persons, but they varied considerably in size. Accompanying each unit was a map indicating its boundaries. Thus, once the households of the state were identified by county of residence, they were further divided into the three types of settlements by means of the geographical units of enumeration districts and block-groups.

For each of the fourteen strata, sample points (enumeration districts and block-groups) were randomly selected to yield the number indicated in Table A.1. Using detailed census maps to which the selected sample points were keyed, interviewers listed *all* the dwellings, single and multiple, in each of the 120 areas throughout North Carolina. The second step was then completed by systematically selecting twelve households within each of the 120 areas. Systematic selection involved randomly choosing one household address as a point of reference and choosing eleven others evenly spaced throughout the area. Twelve households were chosen in anticipation of successfully completing ten household interviews. On the average, two households were expected to be lost due to persistent unavailability of the selected respondent or to refusal to participate in the survey.

In the third step, an interviewer visited each designated household, listed all of the adults in it, and (using a procedure that took into account the number of adults and their ages and gender) chose one adult for interview. If that person was not then available, the interviewer made an appointment to call again.

The sample design and selection procedure used in the "Survey of North Carolina" constituted a multistage area probability sample of households and their adult occupants. Designed to include the major differences in the people of North Carolina, the sample procedures also gave each adult North Carolinian an equal chance of selection for the survey. The only adults excluded from the sample were those living in group quarters (e.g., dormitories), inmates of institutions, and all persons living on military bases.

Successful interviews with 1,130 persons were obtained, for a response rate of 78.5 percent. The interviews, conducted in person in the respondents' homes, averaged ninety minutes in length.

APPENDIX B

Measurement of Key Variables

The survey questions that were used in this analysis are reproduced here, with the recipes for the indexes constructed from them. To the right of the questions I have presented the percentage distributions of some responses for those white respondents who, in answer to question 45, said that they thought of themselves as Southerners (SW), for all other white respondents (OW), and for the blacks in our sample (B).

The Southern whites are, of course, simply those 700+ respondents who formed the basis for the analysis presented in chapters 3 to 7, those whites with *high enough* levels of consciousness and identification to believe that there is a group called "Southerners" that includes them. The other white respondents are an odd lot, as their demographic characteristics and, to some extent, their attitudes show. This category comprises migrants, native residents of the South who believe that their values are "un-Southern," and the extremely out-of-touch. It probably contains both the most and least "cosmopolitan" of our respondents.

The "black" respondents (more accurately, nonwhite—92 percent black, most of the rest Indian) present an interesting pattern of responses. In general, they display about the same level of regional consciousness as the Southern whites but a somewhat lower level of regional identification (although still much higher than that of other whites). They hold many of the typical regional stereotypes to about the same extent as white Southerners (although they are less likely to allow that Southerners are more courteous, more generous, or more patriotic than Northerners). They are about as likely as white Southerners (that is, a good deal more likely than the other whites) to voice all of the characteristic regional grievances, *except those that are related to "outside interference."* For instance, although they are as likely as white Southerners to agree that most Northerners look down on Southerners or that Northern industry has been exploiting the South's natural resources, they are much more likely to agree that "there never would have been any progress in the South without outside assistance and pressure" and to disagree that "the South could solve its problems if the rest of the country would leave it alone." Although they articulate many of the South's current grievances to about the same extent as white Southerners, these black respondents emphatically do not share the white South's major historical grievance. Their score on the index of support for Confederate symbols is substantially lower than even that for non-Southern whites. On the other hand, they resemble Southern whites in their expressed interest in Southern history, a history that is as much the legacy of Southern blacks as of Southern whites, of course, unlike the Confederate experience.

There is one respect in which these black respondents are "super-Southern," differing from non-Southern whites in the same way Southern whites do, only more so. They show a strikingly high level, on the average, of the traditional value orientation. Our index of that value orientation includes a racism component, and most of the black respondents dissent strongly from those particular values, but their traditionalism in other respects is so strong that this one note of dissent is overwhelmed in the summary statistics. Racism aside, the values that our index measures are found in their greatest concentration among our black respondents. This should come as no surprise to someone who has examined the demographic variables: the factors that our analysis showed to be linked to traditional values—rural residence, low levels of education and media exposure, absence of travel and residence outside the South—are a good deal more characteristic of black respondents to this survey than of white ones.

I have organized the questions according to whether they are dependent, attitudinal variables (Table B.1, presented chapter by chapter) or measures of the backgrounds and experiences that were found to be related to these attitudes·(Table B.2). All of the questions except those with prefixes of 42 and 63 (e.g., 42.26 and 63.28) were read to respondents verbatim by the interviewers. Questions in the 42 and 63 series were presented to respondents as two separate "card sorts": cards with the statements on them were shuffled and then presented one at a time to respondents, who placed them on a board with seven spaces ranging from "strongly disagree" (0) to "strongly agree" (6). (A sizable minority of respondents whose reading abilities were not up to this task had the questions read to them by our interviewers.) The question numbers correspond to their positions in the interview schedule (too lengthy in its entirety to be reproduced here, but available from the data library of the Institute for Research in Social Science, University of North Carolina, Chapel Hill).

There were, all told, 740 white Southern respondents, 162 other whites, and 222 blacks. In general, the percentages displayed are based on somewhat smaller Ns because those respondents for whom no answer was recorded (and, in a few cases, those who replied "don't know" or who were not asked a question contingent on some previous response) were excluded from the computation.

Table B.1. Dependent Variables, by Chapter

Chapter 2

45. Some people around here think of themselves as Southerners; others
    do not. How about you—would you say that you are a Southerner
    or not?

	SW	OW	B
1. Yes, a Southerner (ASK 45a.)	100%	—%	73%
2. No, not a Southerner (ASK 45d.)	—	72	16
3. Unsure, don't know (ASK 45f.)	—	28	10

45a. Could you tell me why you feel that way?

45d. Is that because you haven't lived in the South long, or is there
     some other reason?

45f. If you *had to choose*, would you say that you are a Southerner or
     a non-Southerner?

Chapter 3

Consciousness Index. Summed responses to questions 45c and 109,
   scored as indicated.

Index score	SW	OW	B
Low 0	11%	*	10%
1	26	*	25
2	25	*	29
3	20	*	21
High 4	18	*	15

*Index undefined for non-Southerners.

45c. How often do you think of yourself as a Southerner? Very often,
     sometimes, or hardly at all?

	SW	OW	B
1. Very often (2)	35%	*	31%
2. Sometimes (1)	25	*	23
3. Hardly at all (0)	38	*	41
8. Don't know	2	*	4

*Not asked of non-Southerners.

109. How much thought would you say you have given to the South and to Southerners before today? Quite a lot, some, only a little, or almost none?

	SW	OW	B
1. Quite a lot (2)	29%	25%	30%
2. Some (1)	33	27	31
3. Only a little (1)	19	18	19
4. Almost none (0)	17	27	17
8. Don't know	1	4	3

44. How much interest would you say you have in how Southerners as a whole are getting along in this country? Do you have a good deal of interest in it, some interest, or not much interest at all?

	SW	OW	B
1. Good deal of interest	52%	27%	41%
2. Some interest	36	50	39
3. Not much at all	9	19	16
8. Don't know	3	4	4

46. What about the South as a place to live. What would you say are the best things about the South as a place to live?

47. What would you say are the worst things about the South as a place to live?

48. Over the years there has been much talk about the "Southern way of life." Do you think there is a different way of life in the South or is it similar to the way of life in other sections of the country?

	SW	OW	B
1. There is a different way of life (ASK 48a.)	55%	44%	38%
2. No, there is not a different way of life	35	42	41
3. Unsure	4	5	10
8. Don't know	6	9	11

48a. All in all, what would you say is the most important difference between the South and the rest of the country?

Stereotyping Index. Summed responses to questions 49a–49j, with
stereotypic response scored +2, no difference or don't know scored
+1, and counterstereotypic response scored 0.

Index score	SW	OW	B
Low (0–9)	3%	5%	6%
Medium (10–14)	44	54	60
High (15–20)	54	40	33

49. Now I'm going to read you some words that people use to describe
other people. I'm going to ask you whether each word applies more
to Northerners or to Southerners. (SYNONYMS SUPPLIED IF
NECESSARY.)

	SW	OW	B
49a. Courteous (POLITE)			
*Southerners	73%	57%	51%
Northerners	4	10	19
No difference	16	22	22
Don't know	7	11	8
49b. Religious			
*Southerners	60%	54%	65%
Northerners	4	11	5
No difference	23	24	23
Don't know	13	11	6
49c. Industrious (HARD-WORKING)			
Southerners	34%	21%	49%
*Northerners	32	42	25
No difference	25	26	19
Don't know	9	11	7
49d. Aggressive (GO-GETTERS/PUSHY)			
Southerners	16%	13%	25%
*Northerners	57	55	46
No difference	16	18	17
Don't know	11	14	12
49e. Patriotic (LOVE OF ONE'S COUNTRY)			
*Southerners	57%	33%	39%
Northerners	3	11	19
No difference	30	39	26
Don't know	10	16	15

49f. Sophisticated

	SW	OW	B
Southerners	13%	11%	12%
*Northerners	52	47	53
No difference	19	22	20
Don't know	16	20	14

49g. Slow

*Southerners	70%	63%	71%
Northerners	5	4	5
No difference	15	17	14
Don't know	10	15	9

49h. Materialistic

Southerners	15%	14%	20%
*Northerners	38	38	39
No difference	28	26	21
Don't know	19	22	20

49i. Generous

*Southerners	73%	50%	61%
Northerners	2	11	16
No difference	17	28	17
Don't know	7	11	7

49j. Loyal to family

*Southerners	60%	47%	58%
Northerners	1	5	8
No difference	28	33	23
Don't know	11	15	11

*Stereotypic response.

Traditional Value Orientation Index. Responses to items below were scored from 0 to 6, as indicated. Item scores were added to give subscale scores; subscale scores were then standardized by subtracting subscale mean and dividing by subscale standard deviation (mean and standard deviation for total sample). Subscale scores were added to give total scale score, dichotomized at zero for presentation here.

	SW	OW	B
Traditional Value Orientation			
High (>0)	58%	41%	68%
Low (<0)	42	59	32

Authoritarianism Subscale

63.28. Any good leader should be strict with people under him in order to gain their respect.

		SW	OW	B
Strongly disagree	0	3%	3%	4%
	1	15	20	12
	2	8	18	9
Undecided	3	7	9	12
	4	19	19	16
	5	38	28	36
Strongly agree	6	10	4	11

63.33. The most important thing to teach children is absolute obedience to their parents.

		SW	OW	B
Strongly disagree	0	5%	7%	3%
	1	16	24	9
	2	12	15	8
Undecided	3	5	4	3
	4	14	17	11
	5	36	24	42
Strongly agree	6	14	10	23

63.35. No decent man can respect a woman who has sex relations before marriage.

		SW	OW	B
Strongly disagree	0	12%	19%	17%
	1	34	32	31
	2	11	12	12
Undecided	3	10	10	10
	4	7	4	7
	5	18	14	17
Strongly agree	6	8	8	5

Traditional Sex-role Ideology Subscale

63.32. It's somehow unnatural to place a woman in positions of authority over men.

		SW	OW	B
Strongly disagree	0	7%	14%	9%
	1	21	29	18
	2	13	14	9
Undecided	3	8	9	14
	4	16	10	11
	5	29	18	31
Strongly agree	6	6	6	7

63.36. Some equality in marriage is a good thing, but by and large the husband ought to have the main say-so in family matters.

		SW	OW	B
Strongly disagree	0	4%	8%	2%
	1	12	13	8
	2	9	12	7
Undecided	3	4	1	6
	4	16	11	12
	5	41	40	42
Strongly agree	6	14	15	24

Familism Subscale

63.31. Only a relative can be depended on to help you out when you are in trouble.

		SW	OW	B
Strongly disagree	0	23%	23%	17%
	1	54	48	38
	2	9	8	12
Undecided	3	3	2	5
	4	4	6	8
	5	5	9	16
Strongly agree	6	2	5	3

63.38. A person ought to find a job near his parents, even if that means losing a good job elsewhere.

		SW	OW	B
Strongly disagree	0	32%	40%	26%
	1	53	45	40
	2	7	8	13
Undecided	3	3	—	6
	4	2	2	6
	5	2	5	7
Strongly agree	6	1	—	3

Localism Subscale

63.11. Even if it means paying a little bit more, Southerners should take their business to locally-owned companies.

		SW	OW	B
Strongly disagree	0	4%	5%	5%
	1	24	29	22
	2	14	16	12
Undecided	3	14	22	28
	4	13	9	8
	5	27	15	23
Strongly agree	6	3	4	3

63.30. I have greater respect for a man who is well-established in his hometown than a man who is widely known, but who has no local roots.

		SW	OW	B
Strongly disagree	0	4%	4%	2%
	1	16	25	13
	2	8	16	6
Undecided	3	18	23	20
	4	15	8	14
	5	33	22	38
Strongly agree	6	7	2	8

Fatalism Subscale

42.25. Things just happen to me.

		SW	OW	B
Strongly disagree	0	11%	12%	6%
	1	27	33	20
	2	10	8	9
Undecided	3	18	16	20
	4	8	8	12
	5	21	16	25
Strongly agree	6	5	7	8

42.26. Life is essentially a game of chance.

		SW	OW	B
Strongly disagree	0	15%	12%	8%
	1	26	28	16
	2	8	11	6
Undecided	3	9	14	17
	4	13	10	14
	5	25	17	32
Strongly agree	6	5	8	7

42.28. I am happiest when I don't have to make decisions.

		SW	OW	B
Strongly disagree	0	9%	14%	9%
	1	31	34	17
	2	12	9	13
Undecided	3	7	9	11
	4	10	12	13
	5	25	14	28
Strongly agree	6	7	7	8

Resistance to Innovation Subscale

63.27. It generally works out best to keep on doing things the way they have been done before.

		SW	OW	B
Strongly disagree	0	11%	18%	12%
	1	40	42	29
	2	18	16	16
Undecided	3	10	7	13
	4	8	6	10
	5	11	9	19
Strongly agree	6	2	2	2

63.34. People who question the old and accepted ways of doing things usually just end up causing trouble.

		SW	OW	B
Strongly disagree	0	7%	10%	9%
	1	31	40	20
	2	16	8	14
Undecided	3	15	14	13
	4	9	14	16
	5	18	13	23
Strongly agree	6	3	4	4

Racism Subscale

42.05. The public schools should *not* be integrated.

		SW	OW	B
Strongly disagree	0	10%	22%	33%
	1	27	31	35
	2	11	9	5
Undecided	3	13	11	8
	4	7	5	3
	5	18	13	10
Strongly agree	6	15	9	6

42.13. I would not mind if a family of a different color moved next door to me, just so long as they acted like good neighbors.

		SW	OW	B
Strongly disagree	6	14%	11%	2%
	5	19	10	2
	4	6	4	—
Undecided	3	11	3	3
	2	12	10	6
	1	30	43	57
Strongly agree	0	8	19	30

42.05. Integration of the schools is doing more harm than good.

		SW	OW	B
Strongly disagree	0	7%	13%	19%
	1	15	18	40
	2	8	12	10
Undecided	3	11	16	12
	4	10	12	5
	5	28	18	12
Strongly agree	6	22	13	3

42.24. In the long run, integration of the schools will be best for everyone.

		SW	OW	B
Strongly disagree	6	17%	12%	4%
	5	22	12	5
	4	7	6	3
Undecided	3	16	15	12
	2	9	9	6
	1	22	35	46
Strongly agree	0	5	12	25

63.19. The *best thing* about the Southern way of life was racial segregation.

		SW	OW	B
Strongly disagree	0	17%	28%	31%
	1	35	32	29
	2	11	8	9
Undecided	3	15	17	11
	4	7	2	6
	5	10	9	12
Strongly agree	6	5	4	3

Chapter 4

Identification Index. Summed responses to questions 43, 51, and 52, scored as indicated.

Index score		SW	OW	B
Low	0	1% ·	6%	4%
	1	—	7	3
	2	16	50	36
	3	10	14	10
	4	31	19	30
	5	21	4	8
High	6	21	—	9

43. Some people in the South feel they have a lot in common with other Southerners, but others we talk to don't feel this way. How about you? Would you say you feel pretty close to Southerners in general, or that you don't feel much closer to them than you do to other people?

	SW	OW	B
1. Feel closer to Southerners (2)	65%	15%	46%
2. No closer than to others (0)	32	72	49
3. Feel closer to non-Southerners (volunteered) (0)	—	4	1
8. Don't know, can't say (0)	2	8	4

51. Suppose that you are the manager of a company that must hire a scientist. Two persons apply; one born and educated in the North, the other born and educated in the South. If they were equally qualified, which would you prefer, the Northerner or the Southerner?

	SW	OW	B
1. Northerner (0)	4%	17%	14%
2. Southerner (2)	46	17	34
3. Wouldn't care (volunteered) (1)	34	45	34
4. It depends (1)	10	13	11
8. Don't know (1)	6	8	8

51a. Why did you choose the Northerner [Southerner]?

52. Suppose that two good men are running for Congress in your district, but one of them was born and raised in the South, the other born and raised in the North. If each man had moved to the district five years ago, which one would you favor?

	SW	OW	B
1. Northerner (0)	2%	10%	15%
2. Southerner (2)	45	25	26
3. Wouldn't care (volunteered) (1)	27	36	27
4. It depends (1)	20	14	21
8. Don't know (1)	7	14	12

52a. Why did you choose the Northerner [Southerner]?

Chapter 5

54. Some people say Northerners are doing better economically nowadays than Southerners. Do you think Northerners are doing better, worse, or about the same as Southerners?

	SW	OW	B
1. Better	28%	27%	26%
2. Worse	4	4	5
3. Same	55	50	55
8. Don't know	13	19	14

54a. Why do you think that is?

63.16. The South is or soon will be as progressive as any other region of the country.

		SW	OW	B
Strongly disagree	0	1%	1%	3%
	1	4	3	4
	2	4	7	5
Undecided	3	15	22	21
	4	15	14	20
	5	51	44	39
Strongly agree	6	9	8	7

55. Some people say that Northerners have more power in Washington than is fair. Do you think Northerners have more power than is fair, less than is fair, or about the right amount?

	SW	OW	B
1. More than is fair	39%	24%	16%
2. Less than is fair	1	5	1
3. About the right amount	39	52	56
8. Don't know	21	19	27

57. Two judges, Judge Haynesworth and Judge Carswell, were nominated for the Supreme Court and later turned down by the Senate. Some people say they were turned down because they were Southerners, others say this had nothing to do with it. Do you think they were turned down because they were Southerners?

	SW	OW	B
1. Yes	38%	22%	20%
2. No	31	48	46
3. Other response	3	4	2
4. Don't know	28	26	32

Grievance Index. Summed responses for items 63.01 to 63.26 below, scored agree = 2, undecided = 1, disagree = 0 (except item 63.15, where agree = 0 and disagree = 2).

Index score	SW	OW	B
High (15+)	30%	13%	23%
(12–14)	21	18	13
(8–11)	29	26	40
Low (0–7)	20	43	23

63.01. Most Northerners look down on Southerners.

		SW	OW	B
Strongly disagree	0	3%	8%	4%
	1	22	36	16
	2	11	11	6
Undecided	3	15	14	23
	4	16	15	13
	5	24	10	32
Strongly agree	6	8	6	5

63.02. Most of the things which happen to the South are the result of forces outside the South over which Southerners have little control.

		SW	OW	B
Strongly disagree	0	3%	5%	7%
	1	20	31	17
	2	12	12	16
Undecided	3	22	28	30
	4	15	11	11
	5	23	10	16
Strongly agree	6	5	3	2

63.03. Northern industry has been making a big profit off the South's natural resources, like coal and timber, with very little return to the South.

		SW	OW	B
Strongly disagree	0	2%	4%	2%
	1	13	23	10
	2	8	8	9
Undecided	3	33	36	38
	4	13	11	12
	5	26	13	23
Strongly agree	6	5	6	6

63.05. National news programs on radio and television are nearly always unfair to the South.

		SW	OW	B
Strongly disagree	0	5%	6%	7%
	1	31	47	31
	2	18	13	15
Undecided	3	16	19	25
	4	13	9	9
	5	13	5	12
Strongly agree	6	3	2	1

63.08. Books and magazine articles about the South play up its bad points and don't give a fair picture.

		SW	OW	B
Strongly disagree	0	3%	3%	4%
	1	16	29	19
	2	15	16	14
Undecided	3	19	21	27
	4	18	10	14
	5	22	15	18
Strongly agree	6	8	6	4

63.09. The South could solve its problems if the rest of the country would leave it alone.

		SW	OW	B
Strongly disagree	0	4%	9%	11%
	1	20	30	26
	2	12	14	13
Undecided	3	17	18	18
	4	15	12	9
	5	24	13	18
Strongly agree	6	8	4	4

63.15. The South itself is to blame for most of its problems.

		SW	OW	B
Strongly disagree	0	11%	6%	7%
	1	31	23	18
	2	13	13	10
Undecided	3	17	27	18
	4	12	15	14
	5	14	13	25
Strongly agree	6	2	3	8

63.20. The South would be a lot better off if it had won the War Between the States.

		SW	OW	B
Strongly disagree	0	8%	16%	17%
	1	22	31	24
	2	7	8	9
Undecided	3	42	28	34
	4	6	5	4
	5	11	9	8
Strongly agree	6	4	2	3

63.26. The government in Washington doesn't care much what happens to the South.

		SW	OW	B
Strongly disagree	0	8%	12%	12%
	1	37	41	36
	2	14	19	13
Undecided	3	12	12	15
	4	13	4	11
	5	12	7	9
Strongly agree	6	4	4	4

63.04. There would never have been any progress in the South without outside assistance and pressure.

		SW	OW	B
Strongly disagree	0	13%	8%	4%
	1	37	29	13
	2	13	16	7
Undecided	3	19	14	25
	4	9	9	13
	5	8	10	29
Strongly agree	6	2	2	8

63.14. Most Northerners dislike Southerners.

		SW	OW	B
Strongly disagree	0	7%	14%	7%
	1	32	36	30
	2	12	8	14
Undecided	3	20	20	25
	4	11	14	8
	5	14	6	13
Strongly agree	6	3	2	2

63.25. If it could be done without war, the South would be better off as a separate country today.

		SW	OW	B
Strongly disagree	0	27%	42%	24%
	1	42	29	41
	2	6	5	7
Undecided	3	14	13	14
	4	4	1	3
	5	5	6	8
Strongly agree	6	2	4	3

56. One out of every four Americans lives in the South. Should the South be *guaranteed* one out of every four appointments to federal office and to the Supreme Court?

	SW	OW	B
1. Yes, should be	48%	36%	52%
2. No, should not be	38	47	23
8. Don't know	14	17	25

26. In a city where one-third of the people are black, some say that one out of three city employees should be black. Do you approve or disapprove of this idea?

	SW	OW	B
1. Approve	22%	22%	70%
2. Disapprove	42	42	10
3. Depends	9	12	7
4. If qualified	24	20	7
8. Don't know	2	4	6

50. Can you think of any Southerners, living or dead, that you particularly admire?

50a. Who is that? (OBLIGATORY PROBE: Anyone else?)

59. (WHITES ONLY) Do you know if any of your family fought for the Confederacy in the War Between the States?

	SW	OW	B
1. Yes (PROBE: Who was that? Your grandfather, great-grandfather, or what?)			
(Can name on probe)	36%	17%	*
(Cannot name on probe)	3	4	*
2. No	24	47	*
3. Don't know	37	32	*

*Question not asked.

Index of Support for Confederate Symbols. Summed responses to questions 34 and 35 below, scored approve = 6; depends, up to school, or don't know/don't care = 3; disapprove = 0.

Index score	SW	OW	B
Low (0–6)	31%	48%	71%
Medium (9)	16	15	10
High (12)	53	37	20

34. Do you approve of high school bands playing "Dixie" at football games?

	SW	OW	B
1. Approve	86%	75%	41%
2. Disapprove	3	8	20
3. Up to school/students	7	7	18
4. It depends	2	2	7
8. Don't know	3	8	13

35. Do you approve of public schools displaying the Confederate flag?

	SW	OW	B
1. Approve	57%	38%	28%
2. Disapprove	23	38	45
3. Up to school	10	7	10
4. It depends	4	8	6
8. Don't care	6	8	11

Index of Interest in Southern History. Summed responses to questions 63.21 (scored from 0 to 6, with strongly disagree = 0; strongly agree = 6) and 58 (scored: not much, none, or don't know = 0; some interest = 3; great deal = 6).

Index score	SW	OW	B
Low (0–5)	27%	38%	32%
Medium (6–8)	46	52	43
High (9–12)	27	11	25

63.21. There should be more Southern history taught in our schools.

		SW	OW	B
Strongly disagree	0	1%	2%	2%
	1	8	14	8
	2	8	9	4
Undecided	3	20	35	19
	4	20	17	12
	5	36	21	42
Strongly agree	6	7	2	13

58. Would you say you have a great deal of interest in Southern history, some interest, or not much at all?

	SW	OW	B
1. Great deal	30%	15%	23%
2. Some interest	51	61	47
3. Not much	17	17	24
4. None (volunteered)	1	3	3
5. Don't know	1	4	4

Index of Historical Identification. Sum of Index of Support for Confederate Symbols and Index of Interest in Southern History (see above).

Index score	SW	OW	B
Low (0–14)	30%	54%	64%
Medium (15–19)	39	36	26
High (20–24)	31	11	10

Chapter 6

Prejudice Index. Summed responses to the first three items below, scored as indicated.

Index score	SW	OW	B
Low (0–3)	25%	23%	7%
Medium (4–7)	50	58	60
High (9–12)	25	18	33

63.06. Marriages between Northerners and Southerners are just as happy as marriages where both people are from the same part of the country.

		SW	OW	B
Strongly disagree	6	1%	1%	3%
	5	5	4	8
	4	6	1	3
Undecided	3	10	8	13
	2	7	7	8
	1	57	60	55
Strongly agree	0	15	19	11

63.12. People who move to the South from the North never really become Southerners.

		SW	OW	B
Strongly disagree	0	5%	3%	2%
	1	26	21	14
	2	14	17	13
Undecided	3	14	17	13
	4	14	22	29
	5	15	14	12
Strongly agree	6	23	19	25

63.39. I don't like to hear a person with a Northern accent.

		SW	OW	B
Strongly disagree	0	15%	26%	10%
	1	55	44	47
	2	11	10	13
Undecided	3	6	10	14
	4	7	2	6
	5	5	6	9
Strongly agree	6	2	2	1

53. Suppose you had a daughter who wants to marry a young man who was born and raised in the North, but lives here now. Would the fact that he was from the North make you feel good about him, feel bad about him, or wouldn't it make any difference?

	SW	OW	B
1. Feel good about him.	1%	3%	2%
2. Feel bad about him.	2	2	1
3. Wouldn't make any difference.	94	93	92
4. It depends.	2	1	3
8. Don't know.	2	1	2

Table B.2. Principal Background and Experience Variables

1. THE RESPONDENT IS:

	SW	OW	B
(Male)	45%	46%	41%
(Female)	55	54	59

118. IS THE RESPONDENT'S HOUSING UNIT IN:

	SW	OW	B
1. Center of a city or town	5%	3%	12%
2. Not center, but within city limits	41	46	34
3. Suburb of city or town	16	18	3
4. Rural area—mostly non-farm	22	18	24
5. Rural area—mostly farms	17	15	27

94. What was the highest grade you completed in school?

	SW	OW	B
(0–6)	11%	15%	22%
(7–11)	34	24	44
(12)	29	27	20
(Some college or other post–high school)	15	12	8
(College graduate)	6	13	3
(Graduate/professional school)	5	9	2

98c. [ASK OF EMPLOYED]
What kind of work do you do?

	SW	OW	B
(Professional or managerial)	13%	20%	11%
(Clerical or sales)	39	28	11
(Skilled labor, operative)	13	23	11
(Unskilled or service worker)	31	29	62
(Farmer, farm laborer)	3	1	5

108. Most people don't know their exact income for 1971, but would you tell me as best you can what you expect your family's income to be—*before taxes*. Here is a table with income groups on it. Just tell me the letter in front of the group that includes the amount the people living here in your household expect to make in 1971.

	SW	OW	B
A. Up to $1000	3%	5%	10%
B. $1000–1999	5	5	12
C. $2000–2999	6	6	11
D. $3000–3999	7	11	8
E. $4000–4999	6	6	18
F. $5000–7499	18	20	20
G. $7500–9999	18	17	11
H. $10,000–14,999	21	15	8
I. $15,000–24,999	11	13	2
J. $25,000 and up	4	3	1

106. There's quite a bit of talk these days about different social classes. Most people say they belong either to the middle class or to the working class. Do you think of yourself as being in one of these classes? (IF YES: Which class?)

	SW	OW	B
1. Yes			
(middle)	34%	36%	18%
(working)	45	31	62
2. No	20	34	19

38. Did you happen to watch any news on television yesterday or today?

	SW	OW	B
1. Yes	50%	53%	35%
2. No	50	47	65

40. Have you read a newspaper yesterday or today?

	SW	OW	B
1. Yes	76%	65%	48%
2. No	24	35	52

41. Have you been to a public library in the last year?

	SW	OW	B
1. Yes	31%	43%	27%
2. No	69	57	73

84. Now I'd like to ask you all the places you've lived during your life. First, where was your family living when you were born?

	SW	OW	B
(Southern state)	95%	60%	93%
(Border state)	1	4	—
(Other U.S.)	4	36	7
(Foreign)	—	—	—

How long did you live at that address? Where did you move to next? How long did you live there? Now let's go through all the other places you've lived and how long you've lived there.

	SW	OW	B
(Have lived outside South)	14%	41%	18%
(Never lived outside South)	86	59	82

95. Have you attended school outside of the South? (IF YES: How many years?)

	SW	OW	B
(None outside South)	90%	60%	91%
(Less than a year)	2	1	1
(1–5 years outside)	4	6	3
(6 or more years)	3	34	5

88. What is the longest distance you have ever traveled from your place of residence? [PLACE RECORDED AND DISTANCE ESTIMATED]

	SW	OW	B
(Less than 200 miles)	3%	7%	12%
(200–499 miles)	16	12	20
(500 miles or more)	81	81	68

Exposure Index. Constructed from items 84, 88, and 95 above. Low exposure = Southern-born and have not traveled more than 500 miles from home. Traveled in North = Southern-born and have not lived outside South but have traveled more than 500 miles from home. Lived in North = Southern-born and have not gone to school outside South for more than a year but have lived outside South. Extensive exposure = Northern-born or have gone to school outside South for a year or more.

	SW	OW	B
Low exposure	19%	19%	31%
Traveled in North	62	30	48
Lived in North	8	7	11
Extensive exposure	11	45	10

NOTE: The measure of exposure used in Figures 3.1 and 6.1 was constructed somewhat differently. See notes 1–4 to Figure 3.1.

BIBLIOGRAPHY

Abramson, Harold J. "Assimilation and Pluralism." In *The Harvard Encyclopedia of American Ethnic Groups*, edited by Stephan Thernstrom. Cambridge: Harvard University Press, 1980.

Alther, Lisa. *Original Sins*. New York: Alfred A. Knopf, 1981.

Barth, Fredrik, ed. *Ethnic Groups and Boundaries: The Social Organization of Cultural Difference*. Boston: Little, Brown and Company, 1969.

Bertrand, Alvin L. "The Emerging Rural South: A Region under 'Confrontation' by Mass Society." *Rural Sociology* 31 (1966): 449–57.

Blount, Roy, Jr. "C'mon, They're Not All Dumber Than Two-Dollar Dogs!" *TV Guide*, 2 February 1980, pp. 4–8.

Blumer, Herbert. "Race Prejudice as a Sense of Group Position." *Pacific Sociological Review* 1 (1958): 3–7.

Botsch, Robert. *We Shall Not Overcome: Populism and Southern Blue-Collar Workers*. Chapel Hill: University of North Carolina Press, 1980.

Brand, Jack. *The National Movement in Scotland*. London: Routledge & Kegan Paul, 1978.

Broom, Leonard, and Glenn, Norval. "Negro-White Differences in Reported Attitudes and Behavior." *Sociology and Social Research* 50 (1966): 187–200.

Campbell, Angus; Converse, Philip; Miller, Warren; and Stokes, Donald. *The American Voter: An Abridgement*. New York: John Wiley & Sons, 1964.

Caplovitz, David, and Levy, Harry. "Inter-religious Dating among College Students." Research report, Bureau of Applied Social Research, Columbia University, 1965.

Coleman, James. "Relational Analysis: The Study of Social Organization with Survey Methods." *Human Organization* 17 (1958): 28–36.

Coser, Lewis. *The Functions of Social Conflict*. New York: The Free Press of Glencoe, 1964.

Deutsch, Karl. *Nationalism and Social Communication*. Cambridge, Mass.: Technology Press, 1953.

Gans, Herbert J. "Symbolic Ethnicity: The Future of Ethnic Groups and Cultures in America." *Ethnic and Racial Studies* 2 (1979): 1–20.

Garreau, Joel. *The Nine Nations of North America*. Boston: Houghton Mifflin Company, 1981.

Geertz, Clifford. "The Integrated Revolution." In *Old Societies and New Societies*, edited by Clifford Geertz. New York: The Free Press of Glencoe, 1963.

Glenn, Norval D. "Massification vs. Differentiation: Some Trend Data from National Surveys." *Social Forces* 46 (1967): 172–80.

———. "Recent Trends in Inter-category Differences in Attitudes." *Social Forces* 52 (1974): 395–401.

Glenn, Norval D., and Simmons, J. L. "Are Regional Cultural Differences Diminishing?" *Public Opinion Quarterly* 31 (1967): 172–80.

Gould, Peter R., and White, Rodney. *Mental Maps*. Harmondsworth, U.K.: Penguin Books, 1974.

Gouldner, Alvin W. "Cosmopolitans and Locals: Toward an Analysis of Latent Social Roles—I." *Administrative Science Quarterly* 2 (1957–58): 281–306.

Gouldner, Alvin W., and Peterson, Richard A. *Notes on Technology and the Moral Order*. Indianapolis: Bobbs-Merrill, 1962.

Grasmick, Harold. "Social Change and the Wallace Movement in the South." Ph.D. dissertation, Department of Sociology, University of North Carolina, Chapel Hill, 1973.

Greeley, Andrew M. *Ethnicity in the United States: A Preliminary Reconnaissance*. New York: John Wiley & Sons, 1974.

Hackney, Sheldon. "Southern Violence." *American Historical Review* 74 (1969): 906–25.

Hamilton, David L., ed. *Cognitive Processes in Stereotyping and Intergroup Behavior*. Hillsdale, N.J.: Lawrence Erlbaum Associates, 1981.

Harding, John; Proshansky, Harold; Kutner, Bernard; and Chein, Isidor. "Prejudice and Ethnic Relations." In *The Handbook of Social Psychology*, edited by Gardner Lindzey and Elliot Aronson. 2d ed., vol. 5. Reading, Mass.: Addison-Wesley Publishing Company, 1969.

Harvey, John H.; Ickes, William; and Kidd, Robert F., eds. *New Direc-*

tions in Attribution Research. 2 vols. Hillsdale, N.J.: Lawrence Erlbaum Associates, 1976–78.

Hero, Alfred O., Jr. *The Southerner and World Affairs.* Baton Rouge: Louisiana State University Press, 1965.

Hyman, Herbert H. *Secondary Analysis of Sample Surveys: Principles, Procedures, and Potentialities.* New York: John Wiley & Sons, 1972.

Hyman, Herbert H., and Sheatsley, Paul B. "Some Reasons Why Information Campaigns Fail." *Public Opinion Quarterly* 11 (1947): 412–23.

Hyman, Herbert H.; Wright, Charles R.; and Reed, John Shelton. *The Enduring Effects of Education.* Chicago: University of Chicago Press, 1975.

Hyman, Herbert H., and Singer, Eleanor, eds. *Readings in Reference Group Theory and Research.* New York: The Free Press, 1968.

Isaacs, Harold R. *Idols of the Tribe: Group Identity and Political Change.* New York: Harper & Row, 1975.

Janowitz, Morris. *The Professional Soldier: A Social and Political Portrait.* New York: The Free Press, 1960.

Katz, Daniel, and Braley, Kenneth. "Racial Stereotypes of One Hundred College Students." *Journal of Abnormal and Social Psychology* 28 (1933): 280–90.

Keyes, Charles F. "The Dialectics of Ethnic Change." In *Ethnic Change*, edited by Charles F. Keyes. Seattle: University of Washington Press, 1981.

Killian, Lewis. *White Southerners.* New York: Random House, 1970.

Lazarsfeld, Paul F., and Merton, Robert K. "Friendship as a Social Process: A Substantive and Methodological Analysis." In *Freedom and Control in Modern Society*, edited by Morroe Berger, Theodore Abel, and Charles H. Page. New York: D. Van Nostrand Company, 1954.

Lewin, Kurt. *Field Theory in Social Science: Selected Theoretical Papers.* New York: Harper & Brothers, 1951.

Lippmann, Walter. *Public Opinion.* New York: Harcourt, Brace and Company, 1922.

Lipscomb, Lafayette. "Parental Influence in the Development of Black Children's Racial Self-Esteem." Ph.D. dissertation, Department of Sociology, University of North Carolina, Chapel Hill, 1974.

Lyman, Stanford M., and Douglass, William A. "Ethnicity: Strategies of Collective and Individual Impression Management." *Social Research* 40 (1973): 344–65.

McKern, Sharon. *Redneck Mothers, Good Ol' Girls, and Other Southern Belles: A Celebration of the Women of Dixie*. New York: The Viking Press, 1979.

Merton, Robert K. *Social Theory and Social Structure*. Rev. ed. Glencoe, Ill.: The Free Press, 1957.

Odum, Howard W. *The Way of the South*. New York: Macmillan Co., 1947.

Oliver, Pamela. "Measuring Southern Separatism." Seminar paper, Department of Sociology, University of North Carolina, Chapel Hill, undated.

Park, Robert. "The Concept of Social Distance." *Journal of Applied Sociology* 8 (1924): 339–44.

Phillips, Ulrich B. "The Central Theme of Southern History." *American Historical Review* 34 (1928): 30–43.

Pierce, Robert M. "Jimmy Carter and the New South: The View from New York." In *Perspectives on the American South: An Annual Review of Politics, Culture, and Society*, edited by J. S. Reed and Merle Black. vol. 2. New York: Gordon & Breach Science Publishers, 1983.

Pinard, Maurice. *The Rise of a Third Party: A Study in Crisis Politics*. Englewood Cliffs, N.J.: Prentice-Hall, 1971.

Potter, David. *The South and the Sectional Conflict*. Baton Rouge: Louisiana State University Press, 1968.

Reed, John Shelton. *The Enduring South: Subcultural Persistence in Mass Society*. Chapel Hill: University of North Carolina Press, 1974.

———. "For Dixieland: The Sectionalism of *I'll Take My Stand*." In *A Band of Prophets: The Vanderbilt Agrarians after Fifty Years*, edited by Walter Sullivan and William Havard. Baton Rouge: Louisiana State University Press, 1982.

———. *One South: An Ethnic Approach to Regional Culture*. Baton Rouge: Louisiana State University Press, 1982.

———. "Southerners." In *The Harvard Encyclopedia of American Ethnic Groups*, edited by Stephan Thernstrom. Cambridge: Harvard University Press, 1980.

Rosenberg, Morris. "The Dissonant Religious Context and Emotional Disturbance." *American Journal of Sociology* 68 (1962): 1–10.

Rosenberg, Morris, and Simmons, Roberta G. *Black and White Self-*

Esteem. New York: American Sociological Association, 1971.

Royce, Anya Peterson. *Ethnic Identity: Strategies of Diversity*. Bloomington: Indiana University Press, 1982.

Runciman, W. G. *Relative Deprivation and Social Justice: A Study of Attitudes to Social Inequality in Twentieth-Century England*. Harmondsworth, U.K.: Penguin Books, 1974.

Sherer, Robert. "I'm from Dixie, Too." Paper presented at Annual Meeting of the Southwestern Social Science Association, 1981.

Shibutani, Tamotsu. "On the Personification of Adversaries." In *Human Nature and Collective Behavior: Papers in Honor of Herbert Blumer*, edited by Tamotsu Shibutani. Englewood Cliffs, N.J.: Prentice-Hall, 1970.

Simpson, Richard. "Friendship Cliques in the United States Air Force Wings." Technical Report no. 3, Air Force Base Project, Institute for Research in Social Science, University of North Carolina, Chapel Hill, undated.

Tindall, George. *The Ethnic Southerners*. Baton Rouge: Louisiana State University Press, 1977.

———. "The Sunbelt Snow Job." *Houston Review* 1 (1979): 3–13.

Triandis, Harry C. *Attitude and Attitude Change*. New York: John Wiley & Sons, 1971.

———. "Frequency of Contact and Stereotyping." *Journal of Personality and Social Psychology* 7 (1967): 316–28.

Turner, John C., and Giles, Howard, eds. *Intergroup Behavior*. Chicago: University of Chicago Press, 1981.

Twelve Southerners. *I'll Take My Stand: The South and the Agrarian Tradition*. New York: Harper Torchbooks, 1962.

Vallee, Frank G. "Regionalism and Ethnicity: The French-Canadian Case." In *Perspectives on Regions and Regionalism, and Other Papers*, edited by B. Y. Card. Edmonton, Alta.: Western Association of Sociology and Anthropology, 1969.

Vance, Rupert B. *Human Geography of the South*. Chapel Hill: University of North Carolina Press, 1932.

Vanneman, Reeve D., and Pettigrew, Thomas. "Race and Relative Deprivation in the Urban United States." *Race* 13 (1972): 461–86.

Vanover, J.R. "Redneck Mammas and Blue Collar Workers." *Southern Partisan*, Fall 1981, pp. 27–28.

———. "The Useful South." *Southern Partisan*, January 1980, pp. 37–38.

Waters, Tom. "Old Times There Are Not Forgotten." Seminar paper,

Curriculum in American Studies, University of North Carolina, Chapel Hill, 1981.

Weber, Max. "Class, Status, and Party." In *Class, Status, and Power: A Reader in Social Stratification*, edited by Reinhard Bendix and S. M. Lipset. Glencoe, Ill.: The Free Press, 1953.

Williams, John E., and Morland, J. Kenneth. *Race, Color, and the Young Child*. Chapel Hill: University of North Carolina Press, 1976.

Wilson, Charles R. *Baptized in Blood: The Religion of the Lost Cause, 1865–1920*. Athens: University of Georgia Press, 1980.

Wood, Gail. "The Images of Southern Males and Females." Senior honors paper, Department of Sociology, University of North Carolina, Chapel Hill, 1973.

Woodward, C. Vann. *The Burden of Southern History*. Rev. ed. Baton Rouge: Louisiana State University Press, 1968.

INDEX

For Reference

Not to be taken from this room